CLASSIC CHILDREN'S GAMES

CLASSIC CHILDREN'S GAMES

Ages 2 to 10

Vivienne Sernaqué

A DELL TRADE PAPERBACK

A DELL TRADE PAPERBACK
Published by
Dell Publishing
a division of
The Bantam Doubleday Dell Publishing Group, Inc.
666 Fifth Avenue
New York, New York 10103

ISBN: 0-440-50024-9

Printed in the United States of America

Published simultaneously in Canada

October 1988

10 9 8 7 6 5 4 3 2

MV

For Eva, who started it all

Contents

4·Classic Games for Ages Eight to Ten 105

CLASSIC CHILDREN'S GAMES

1

. . . .

Classic Games for Ages Two to Four

The world of games is a magical place in childhood. For the two-to four-year-old, game time is reliable fun when it isn't too scary (except for the occasional excitement of a chase, or a wicked wolf), when it operates within known guidelines, when it's rhythmic and lively, when it contains an element of surprise or change of pace, and, as all parents know, when it can be repeated a zillion times!

Though most of us know the fast-food versions of many of the games that follow, knowing a little more about them will surely enrich you and your child's play—and perhaps suggest ways to tailor the games to suit your child's readiness. As you will see, many of these games are like those undershirts that somehow stretch to fit your child forever!

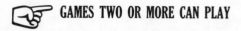 **GAMES TWO OR MORE CAN PLAY**

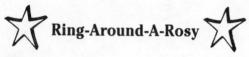 **Ring-Around-A-Rosy**

Number of Players: 2 or more
Equipment: None

LORE

This is such a basic childhood game that it would be presumptuous to assume that anyone *doesn't* know it, or at least some version of it. There also exist different versions of the game's origin. Probably the neatest and most widely known explanation for "Ring-a-ring-o-roses" recalls the Great Plague of London, which dates back to 1664. A "rosy" rash was supposedly a symptom, a "pocketful of posies" (special herbs) were carried to ward off the evil disease, "A-tishoo" was the sneezing that may also have been a symptom, or in the version I learned as a child, "Ashes" was thought to be either the ashen color of the terminally ill, or the cremated bodies of the unfortunate dead. Of course, "we all fall down" is self-explanatory. Nice rhyme, right? Well, you don't have to believe any of this as there seems to be no documentation to substantiate this theory, likely as it may seem. In fact, no record of the words to this game appears in children's literature before 1881, although New Bedford, Massachusetts, had a version in 1790.

A much happier connection is the old-world belief that gifted children had the capability of laughing roses. Foreign and nineteenth-century versions described curtseys and bows in place of falling down, the game itself having to do with drama and singing. Take your choice, add your own interpretation, or just play it with your child for fun!

HOW TO PLAY
• Children hold hands and walk in a circle while singing rhyme.
On the last verse, everyone falls.

Ring around a rosy
A pocketful of posies
Ashes, Ashes
We all fall down!

Variations
Ring-A-Ring o' Roses
A pocket full of posies
A-tishoo! A-tishoo!
We all fall down.

A ring, a ring o' roses,
A pocket full of posies,
Ash-a! Ash-a!
All stand still.

The king has sent his daughter
To fetch a pail of water,
Ash-a! Ash-a!
All bow down.

The bird upon the steeple
Sits high above the people,
Ash-a! Ash-a!
All kneel down.

The wedding bells are ringing,
The boys and girls are singing,
Ash-a! Ash-a!
All fall down.

Well known also is a follow-up verse in which the children jump up again:

> The cows are in the meadow,
> Lying fast asleep.
> Thunder, lightning,
> We all jump up.

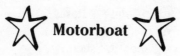

Motorboat

Number of Players: 2
Equipment: None

LORE
No historical claims are to be made for this one. However, I do promise you that from the time your child can walk with your help, he or she will delight in playing Motorboat. The hardest part will be convincing him or her to rest as you both stagger around dizzily. Sounds like fun, doesn't it? P.S. Play this one on a rug.

SETTING UP
• Hold hands and walk around in a circle.

HOW TO PLAY
• As you walk chant, "Motorboat, motorboat, go so slowly."
• Speed up a little and chant, "Motorboat, motorboat, go so fast. "
• Take the child securely under the armpits and lift the child off the ground, swinging him or her around in a circle as you chant, "Motorboat, motorboat, step on the gas!"
• Sit down between rounds.

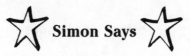 **Simon Says**

Number of Players: 2 or more
Equipment: None

LORE
As they're both tricksters, this Simon could be connected to Simple Simon of nursery-rhyme fame. I remember playing it as a child and having to say "Simple Simon says." In any case, both Simons are fun to have around, and Simon Says works all the way from age two to age ten. Try to have a homogeneous group, though, as varying physical abilities make a difference.

SETTING UP
• One player is Simon. He or she stands facing the rest of the players.
• Players spread out so all have an arm's-length space around them and are able to see Simon clearly.

HOW TO PLAY
• Simon performs any action, such as raising arms, jogging in place, or bending forward, and at the same time instructs the other players to copy the action.
• Simon must, however, say "Simon says" beforehand in order to get the players to do it.
• Simon tries to trick the other players into copying him or her without saying "Simon says." Simon may say "Do this ..." followed by an action. If another player follows, that player is out.

WINNING
• The last player left in the game gets to be Simon next.
• Watch out for the wise guy who says "Simon says jump up!" then disqualifies all the players when they land.

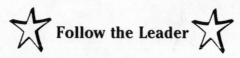

Follow the Leader

Number of Players: up to 10
Equipment: None

LORE
Before the advent of the "toy culture" as we know it today, children had to be inventive, ingenious, and often daring in order to amuse themselves and others. Follow the Leader is one of those universal games in which natural leaders emerge, but also it is one in which the importance of being able to follow is not slighted.

Wide-open spaces suit this game perfectly. A mix of ages makes for surprises!

SETTING UP
• Players take turns being the leader. Decide in advance how the transition from one leader to the next is to be accomplished. Some possibilities are: a time limit, when a certain amount of space is covered, once ten "stunts" are performed.
• Players line up behind the leader, leaving an arm's-length space between them.

HOW TO PLAY
• The leader begins by walking forward then does anything he or she feels like doing, the sillier the better. Running, jumping, climbing fences, handstands, cartwheels, hopping, skipping—any and all manner of feats as long as they are amusing and not dangerous.
• Followers must copy the leader's antics.
• Leaders change periodically, and the game continues until the players are bored or exhausted—usually the latter.

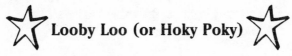

Looby Loo (or Hoky Poky)

Number of Players: 2 or more
Equipment: None

LORE

Looby Loo and Hoky Poky are strikingly similar games with different tunes and slightly different formats. Hoky Poky had a surge of popularity in the 1950s, though Looby Loo is an old English singing game that may have originated as part of religious ritual dating as far back as the Druids.

In the game today, the younger children get to show off not their religious fervor but their knowledge of body parts, and the older ones get to shake it up a little.

HOW TO PLAY

• Players hold hands and form a circle.
• Players sing the first four lines of the song while either skipping or walking in a circle.
• Players then stand in place and continue to sing as they follow the instructions for each verse.
• The refrain is repeated, alternating direction, before each instructional verse.

> Here we dance looby loo
> Here we dance looby light
>
> Here we dance looby loo
> All on a Saturday night.
>
> I put my right hand in
> I put my right hand out

I give my right hand a shake, shake, shake
And turn myself about.

I put my left hand in ...
I put my two hands in ....
I put my right foot in ...
I put my left foot in ...
I put my two feet in ...
I put my right ear in ...
I put my left ear in ...
I put my little head in ...
I put my whole self in ...

Variation

HOKY POKY

• This version dispenses with the circle dance but replaces it with a refrain at the end in which players can invent their own "Hoky Poky" dance to get themselves turned around.
• Any body part is fair game!

I put my left hand in
I take my left hand out
I put my left hand in
And I shake it all about.

I do the Hoky Poky
And I turn myself around
That's what it's all about. (Clap)

I put my right hand in ...
I put my left foot in ...
I put my right foot in ...

I put my head in ...
I put my left side in ...
I put my right side in ...
I put my whole self in ...

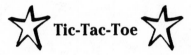 **Tic-Tac-Toe**

Number of Players: 2
Equipment: 2 pencils, paper

LORE
This game is great for children around four years of age who are just discovering concepts such as "three in a row" and "diagonal." When the thrill of discovery is gone, there's still the competitive spirit to be tapped, but once kids really have it down, it may be time to move on—or to teach it to a younger sibling!

SETTING UP
• Draw the figure illustrated on a sheet of paper.
• One player chooses *X*, the other player chooses *O*.

HOW TO PLAY
• The aim of the game is to place three *X*'s or three *O*'s in succession, either horizontally, vertically, or diagonally, before your opponent does the same. In order to do this each player must try not only to get his or her *X*'s or *O*'s in the right places, but also to prevent the other player from accomplishing the same aim.
• *X* always goes first. The player puts an *X* in any of the boxes. *O* then takes a turn, and so on until one or the other has won, or until all spaces are filled and there is no winner.

WINNING
• Some ways in which the game can be won are illustrated.
• *X*'s and *O*'s should trade after each game because *X*'s have an advantage.

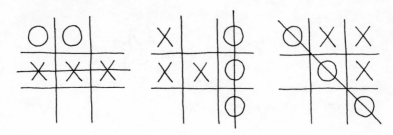

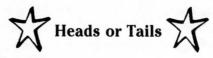 **Heads or Tails**

Number of Players: 2
Equipment: Coin

LORE
In ancient Greece a game called the Game of the Shell was played. It was like tag. One side of a seashell was colored dark (for night), the other was left light (for day). The shell was spun to decide who would be "It." In nineteenth-century America, a flat disc, black on one side, white on the other, was thrown to decide who would be "It." By the time of the Depression, it was called Heads or Tails, and before long a coin replaced the disc—voilà!

As Heads or Tails evolved further, it became the classic way to settle all manner of dispute, from who goes first to who takes out the trash. "I'll flip you for it" is also a handy amusement while waiting on line with your young one—as long as *you* do the flipping.

SETTING UP
• Players agree which side of the coin to be used is "heads" and which is "tails." Bigger coins are easier to use.

HOW TO PLAY
• One player takes the coin and balances it on the side of an index finger. With the thumb of the same hand, he or she then flicks the coin into the air, making it turn over and over. The player catches the coin in the flat palm of the hand and, before looking at the coin, places the palm, with coin, on the back of the other hand and holds it there, coin concealed.
• The other player guesses "heads" or "tails" to indicate which side of the coin he or she thinks will show when the concealing hand is removed.

WINNING
• If a player guesses correctly he or she gets to flip the coin next (or, with a younger child, the satisfaction of guessing correctly!).
• If the player's guess is wrong the coin is flipped and he or she tries again.
• The game is often played the best three out of five, five out of seven, and so on.

 **GAMES FOR MORE THAN TWO**

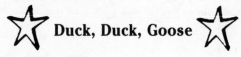 **Duck, Duck, Goose**

Number of Players: 6–8 ideal
Equipment: None

LORE
Is this where the name for that nasty little pinch comes from? Whether it is or not, the combination of suspense, entertainment, and physical activity in this game is hard to beat. It's a perfect party game for a group of young ones, sure to be accompanied by shrieks and laughter.

SETTING UP
• One player is Fox.
• The other players form a circle and face the middle, with Fox outside.

HOW TO PLAY
• Fox walks around the circle gently tapping each child and saying "Duck, duck, duck ..." until he or she taps one child and shouts "Goose!"
• Goose then chases Fox around the circle.

WINNING
• If Goose can catch Fox before Fox reaches the spot in the circle Goose vacated, then Goose resumes his or her place and Fox has to try again.
• If Fox reaches the empty place safely, then Goose becomes Fox for the next round.

Variation

If foxes, ducks, and geese don't happen to strike your fancy, or just to add some diversity, have the child who is "It" call "Hamburger, Hamburger, Hot Dog!" or "Ketchup, Ketchup, Mustard!" or "Dog, Dog, Cat!"

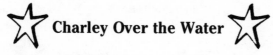

Charley Over the Water

Number of Players: 6–8 ideal
Equipment: None

LORE

Although this game may be unfamiliar to you, a few of the records and tapes for younger children contain the pleasant tune to this rhyme. It was especially popular at the beginning of this century.

SETTING UP

• In order for Charley to have a fair chance at catching someone, you may have to introduce a little discipline during the game, such as having all the children stand up straight on the last word of the rhyme.
• One child is "Charley."
• The other children form a circle around him or her, holding hands.

HOW TO PLAY

• Players sing the rhyme, as they skip around the circle, then squat after the last word. Charley tries to catch one of them before he or she is all the way down.

WINNING
• Whoever is caught must then become Charley for the next round.

> Charley over the water,
> Charley over the sea,
> Charley catch a blackbird,
> Can't catch me.

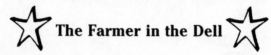

The Farmer in the Dell

Number of Players: 8 or more
Equipment: None

LORE
In case you don't remember, a dell is a small valley. When the players circle around the Farmer, they create a dell for him or her to stand in. This is a charming children's game, and it may be the first time the littlest ones have ever thought about "choosing" another person to be with. Parents of "cheeses" will find *their* feelings injured much more than their child's!

SETTING UP
• One player is chosen to be Farmer.
• With Farmer in the center, players hold hands and form a circle.

HOW TO PLAY
• Players sing the rhyme while walking around Farmer. Farmer points to the player chosen as "Wife," and he or she joins Farmer in the middle as the others continue to sing and walk, still holding hands.

• The game continues, with Wife choosing Child, Child choosing Nurse, and so on, until at last a "Cheese" is chosen, by which time the outside circle will be fairly depleted and the inside crammed with wiggling bodies. Everyone stops to clap and point at the lowly Cheese, who was chosen last.

• The revenge of the Cheese, however, is that he or she gets to be Farmer in the next round.

> The farmer in the dell,
> The farmer in the dell,
> Hey-o, the derry-o,
> The farmer in the dell.
>
> The farmer takes a wife,
> The farmer takes a wife,
> Hey-o, the derry-o,
> The farmer takes a wife.
>
> The wife takes a child,
> The wife takes a child,
> Hey-o, the derry-o,
> The wife takes a child.
>
> The child takes a nurse,
> The child takes a nurse,
> Hey-o, the derry-o,
> The child takes a nurse.
>
> The nurse takes a dog,
> The nurse takes a dog,
> Hey-o, the derry-o,
> The nurse takes a dog.

The dog takes a cat,
The dog takes a cat,
Hey-o, the derry-o,
The dog takes a cat.

The cat takes a rat,
The cat takes a rat,
Hey-o, the derry-o,
The cat takes a rat.

The rat takes a cheese,
The rat takes a cheese,
Hey-o, the derry-o,
The rat takes a cheese.

The cheese stands alone
The cheese stands alone
Hey-o, the derry-o,
The cheese stands alone.

London Bridge

Number of Players: 4 or more
Equipment: None

LORE

This game is such a special favorite that I don't believe
I've ever met anyone who doesn't know at least one verse and the
tune that goes with it as well. As with Ring-Around-A-Rosy, theo-
ries about its origin abound, but unlike that game, it seems
London Bridge isn't actually played as much as it's sung. The

game itself is great fun and, once learned, tends to erupt sponta-
neously in all sorts of situations—our six-year-old still plays it!

Though it would seem obvious from the title that this game is
British in origin—and in fact the original London Bridge dates
back to the twelfth century—similar games have been found
throughout Europe. Rabelais, the great sixteenth-century French
literary figure, mentions the game under the name of Fallen
Bridge. A similar game called Coda Romana was played by the
children of Florence as early as 1328. There were versions in
Spain and in Germany as well. In English writings, it isn't until
1719 that a dance called London Bridge appears. Not long
afterward it was well known and accepted as children's terrain.
One stanza seems to have originated during the time of Henry
VIII (1491–1547): "Take the key and lock her up." This could refer
to Henry having locked not one but two of his wives, Anne Boleyn
and Catherine Howard, in the Tower of London. There were a few
more famous women prisoners in the Tower as well, including
Lady Jane Grey and Elizabeth I. Seems the English have quite a
history of taking the key and locking her up.

SETTING UP
• Two players are chosen to form the bridge. They decide
between themselves who will be "gold" and who will be "silver."
• The two players stand opposite each other, lift their arms,
and hold hands so the other players can pass beneath the arch,
or bridge, that is formed.

HOW TO PLAY
• Players hold on to one another's waist and pass beneath the
arch in a line as they all sing the song.

• At the last word in each stanza, "lady," the "bridge" falls down and tries to trap the player passing underneath.

• If a prisoner is caught, he or she is asked to choose between gold and silver. The prisoner must whisper the answer, then line up behind whomever he or she has chosen.

WINNING
• The winning team is the one with the most players at the end or, in some versions, a Tug-of-War determines the winner. See Tug-of-War (page 118) for the rules.

Variation
For the younger children who haven't the patience to wait until everyone is lined up for the Tug-of-War, the game can be simplified, without any loss of fun, by the following:

• After the word "lady" in each stanza, the "bridge" drops and catches the player passing underneath.

• The "bridge" then swings the prisoner to and fro while singing the "Take the key and lock her up" stanza.

• Once the prisoner is released, he or she can rejoin the line.

• We usually repeat the "lock her up" verse between each main verse to add a little more action.

London Bridge is falling down, falling down, falling down,
London Bridge is falling down, my fair lady.

Build it up with iron bars, iron bars, iron bars,
Build it up with iron bars, my fair lady.

Iron bars will rust away, rust away, rust away,
Iron bars will rust away, my fair lady.

Build it up with needles and pins, needles and pins, needles
    and pins,
Build it up with needles and pins, my fair lady.

Pins and needles bend and break, bend and break, bend
    and break,
Pins and needles bend and break, my fair lady.

Build it up with silver and gold, silver and gold, silver and gold,
Build it up with silver and gold, my fair lady.

Gold and silver I've not got, I've not got, I've not got,
Gold and silver I've not got, my fair lady.

Take the key and lock her up, lock her up, lock her up,
Take the key and lock her up, my fair lady.

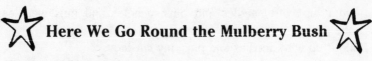

Here We Go Round the Mulberry Bush

Number of Players: 2 to many
Equipment: None

LORE
Young children have always seemed to love the comfort of holding hands and moving rhythmically in a circle. Here is another old but still popular game that, although it may not foster an appreciation of household drudgery, may come in handy when you're bored with Ring-Around-A-Rosy and not quite up for Motorboat.

SETTING UP
• Players form a circle and link hands.

HOW TO PLAY
• For the first stanza players either walk or skip around in a circle, singing the song.
• Players then stop and follow directions in the song as they continue to sing, making up their own motions for each activity.

> Here we go round the mulberry bush,
> The mulberry bush, the mulberry bush.
> Here we go round the mulberry bush,
> So early in the morning.
>
> This is the way we wash our clothes,
> Wash our clothes, wash our clothes.
> This is the way we wash our clothes,
> On a Monday morning.

This is the way we iron our clothes,
Iron our clothes, iron our clothes.
This is the way we iron our clothes,
On a Tuesday morning.

This is the way we scrub our floors,
Scrub our floors, scrub our floors.
This is the way we scrub our floors,
On a Wednesday morning.

This is the way we mend our clothes,
Mend our clothes, mend our clothes.
This is the way we mend our clothes,
On a Thursday morning.

This is the way we sweep the house,
Sweep the house, sweep the house.
This is the way we sweep the house,
On a Friday morning.

We play when our work is done,
Work is done, work is done.
We play when our work is done,
On a Saturday morning.

This is the way we go to church,
Go to church, go to church.
This is the way we go to church,
On a Sunday morning.

I take my rest when my play is done,
Play is done, play is done.
I take my rest when my play is done,
So early in the morning.

2

·· ·

Classic Games for Ages Four to Six

Somewhere around age four, your child will probably be ready for some challenge involving manual dexterity. At the same time, his or her concentration span will begin to lengthen. You'll find your child having fun by satisfying his or her innate drive to "practice" these new skills through play.

Still, growing bodies contain immense amounts of physical energy to be expended in good-time games with friends. The rules keep the activity at a high level without becoming chaotic (sometimes), and socialization and cooperation become welcome by-products of having fun.

 GAMES ONE OR MORE CAN PLAY

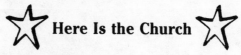 **Here Is the Church**

Number of Players: 1 or more
Equipment: None

LORE
Though this is a good game to show to your younger child, the manual dexterity to actually do it will probably not appear until around age four.

HOW TO PLAY
• Place hands back to back, with fingers spread.
• Interlace fingers, then bend and hold them while turning palms to face each other.
• Thumbs stay upright in front of interlaced fingers with knuckles forming the roof of the church.
• Raise index fingers and press them together to make the church steeple.
• Part thumbs to open the church door.
• Bring backs of hands together, straighten fingers, and wiggle them to show people.
• Separate fingers and rest backs of hands against each other once again. To make the parson walk upstairs, link pinkies, then ring fingers, middles, and index fingers in succession.
• Still holding on, bring the palms together and extend fingers for prayer position.

> Here is the church, and here is the steeple.
> Open the door and here are the people.
> Here is the parson going upstairs,
> And here he is a-saying his prayers.

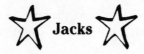

Jacks

Number of Players: 1–4
Equipment: 1 small ball, set of jacks

LORE
The game of Jacks is derived from a primitive form of dice called Knucklebones, first played in Asia Minor, using sheep's knuckles. The game spread to ancient Greece and Rome and through the centuries to many parts of the world. (Figures playing what looks to be Knucklebones, which didn't use a ball, can be seen in a Pompeiian fresco.) In England of 1688 Jacks, or Fivestones, was referred to as an amusement for country boys and girls. Today sheep's knuckles are no longer in use, nor are stones, but rather five small, spiky metal objects that are good for spinning and, of course, a small ball.

SETTING UP
• Players agree on the sequence of turns.
• The first player kneels, squats, or sits in a comfortable position with the ball in hand. He or she then throws the jacks to scatter (not too far) in a manner similar to dice.

HOW TO PLAY
• The player bounces the ball, picks up one jack without moving any of the others, transfers it to the holding hand, and catches the ball with the same hand that bounced it.
• If the player can do this successfully, he or she continues by repeating the sequence with two jacks at a time, then three, four, up to the number of jacks available (the maximum is usually ten). Then the sequence is reversed, with the player picking up ten first, then nine, eight, and on down.

• If the player misses, the next player takes a turn. When it is the first player's turn again, he or she attempts the step that was missed.

WINNING
• The first player to complete the sequence with all the jacks, wins the round.

Variation

FANCIES
• After the initial round, the winner is invited to dream up a harder sequence. For example: The player sets one jack spinning, bounces the ball, picks the jack up before it stops spinning, transfers the jack to holding hand, and catches the ball after only one bounce (called Cherries in the Basket), again only using the hand that bounced the ball.
• The next round may add claps corresponding to the number of jacks to be picked up. The round after that—you're on your own!

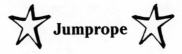

Jumprope

Number of Players: 1 to many
Equipment: Jumprope

LORE
There seem to be a number of "world's oldest games," and jumprope is another one. Historically, after spring planting, festivities were held in which there were songs and jumping contests. It was believed that crops would grow only as high as the planter could jump. Sometime later, in the English countryside of the 1800s, jumpropes were made from hop stems stripped of their leaves. Rope jumping has traditionally been used for answering all manner of questions and telling fortunes, and, as you will see, this superstition is strongly evident in our modern jumprope rhymes: How many times? How many days? Whom will I marry? How long will I live? These, and many other questions, can be determined by rope-jumping prowess, so stay tuned and get out your jumprope.

SETTING UP
• Jumprope is a very versatile game that can be played by one, two, three, or more players.
• When only one child is playing, he or she holds one end of the rope in each hand so that the slack in between is long enough to be pulled comfortably over the player's head but not long enough to drag on the ground once it's turned.
• For two players, one holds each end of the rope and the second player takes his or her place either in front or in back of the first, and jumps along with the first player.
• For three or more players, two players face each other, each holding one end of the jumprope. They synchronize their move-

ments and stand far enough apart so that the rope is swung smoothly in a circle, barely touching the ground as it goes around, with enough room in the center for a player or players to jump.
• Just in case you've forgotten your jumprope terminology, here is a quick refresher:

Back door: When two are playing, the position behind the jumper holding the rope. When three or more are playing, the jumper enters the back door when he or she must jump in as the rope is turning away from him or her.

Bluebells: The rope is swung gently back and forth, usually between two holders—especially good for the younger players.

Double Dutch: For three or more only, this variation uses two ropes, with turners holding one end of each in each hand and turning the ropes alternately, either toward or away from each other.

Front door: When two are playing, the position in front of the jumper holding the rope. When three or more are playing, the jumper enters the front door when he or she must jump in as the rope is turning toward him or her.

Salt, pepper, cider, vinegar: Used as a rhyme in itself, or at the end of a rhyme to speed things up—or to trip a good jumper. Each represents a faster speed of turning the rope. Can also be: Salt, vinegar, mustard, pepper—or perhaps in your town, something else.

HOW TO PLAY
• The rope is swung either by a lone player or by two. The player jumps over (or in) and continues to jump for as long as he or she can, wants to, or as long as it's his or her turn.

• Jumping can be a hop, a two-footed jump, a larger jump followed by a smaller one, or whatever pattern is most comfortable for the jumper. The object is to continue smoothly, without tripping.

• When a player misses, he or she must take the place of one of the turners.

• Players usually chant a popular jumprope rhyme, chant the rhyme and imitate actions in the rhyme, or simply count the number of jumps.

RHYMES
Can you believe that some of these rhymes are still around?

> Cinderella, dressed in yellow
> Went upstairs to kiss a fellow
> By mistake, she kissed a snake
> How many doctors did it take?
> One, two, three, four ...

> Teddy bear, teddy bear,
> Turn around
> Teddy bear, teddy bear,
> Touch the ground
> Teddy bear, teddy bear,
> Tie your shoe
> Teddy bear, teddy bear,
> that will do

Teddy bear, teddy bear,
Go upstairs
Teddy bear, teddy bear,
Say your prayers
Teddy bear, teddy bear,
Dim the light
Teddy bear, teddy bear,
Say goodnight

• For the following rhyme, jump in on your birthday month, then jump out when it comes up again.

All in together, girls.
How is the weather, girls?
January, February, March ...

All out together, girls.
How is the weather, girls?
January, February, March ...

OR

Sunny, sunny weather
All come in together
January, February ...

Rainy, rainy weather
All go out together
January, February ...

• Here's a cheery one.

Apples, peaches, pumpkin pie,
How many days before I die?
1, 2, 3, 4 ...

• And don't let your little innocents trick you into this one.

> My mother sent me to the store,
> And this is what she sent me for:
> Salt, pepper, cider, vinegar.

(On the last line, the rope is turned faster and faster. If a player is still jumping, the line is repeated ever faster until he or she misses.)

• For younger children, jumping in is a hard-learned technique. The following is a good way to start any rhyme with the jumper already in the middle. The rope is swung gently back and forth as the verse is sung. On the word OVER, the rope is brought over the jumper's head, and regular jumping begins.

> Bluebells, cockleshells,
> Evie, ivy, OVER.

• And lest we forget those perennial favorites, the Spanish Dancer and the Lady with the Alligator Purse:

> I went downtown to see Miss Brown
> She gave me a nickel to buy a pickle
> The pickle was sour so I bought a flower
> The flower was dead so I bought some thread
> The thread was thin so I bought a pin
> The pin was sharp so I bought a harp
> And on that harp I played:
> Little Spanish dancer, do the splits
> Little Spanish dancer, give a high kick
> Little Spanish dancer, turn around
> Little Spanish dancer, touch the ground

Here's another version:

> Spanish dancer, do the splits
> Spanish dancer, give a high kick
> Spanish dancer, take a sip of wine
> Close your eyes, and count to nine.
> 1, 2, 3 . . .

> Miss Lucy had a baby
> She named him Tiny Tim
> She put him in the bathtub
> To teach him how to swim

> He drank all the water
> He ate all the soap
> He tried to eat the bathtub
> But it wouldn't fit down his throat

> Miss Lucy called the doctor
> Miss Lucy called the nurse
> Miss Lucy called the Lady
> with the Alligator Purse

> In came the doctor
> In came the nurse
> In came the Lady
> with the Alligator Purse

> "Mumps," said the doctor
> "Measles," said the nurse
> "Nothing," said the Lady
> with the Alligator Purse

Out walked the doctor
Out walked the nurse
Out walked the Lady
with the Alligator Purse

Out came the water
Out came the soap
Out came the bathtub
that wouldn't fit down his throat!

Variations
• When there are a number of players, a game such as One, Two, Three or Follow the Leader will give everyone a chance to participate without long waits.

ONE, TWO, THREE
• The first jumper jumps in, jumps once, and jumps out. The second jumper follows, and so on, until it's the first jumper's turn again. He or she jumps in, jumps twice, and jumps out. The second player follows suit. You get the idea.

FOLLOW THE LEADER
• The first jumper jumps in and does whatever he or she wants (as long as it's relatively short). Other jumpers must follow and copy. Then the second jumper does whatever he or she wants to do, and so the game continues.

☆ Pickup Sticks ☆

Number of Players: 1–4
Equipment: Pickup sticks (usually 50 per package)

LORE

Pickup Sticks, also called Jackstraws and Spellicans, probably originated in China, where sets of sticks were made of ivory and sometimes elaborately carved with heads of horses, birds in nests, and other decorations. Alas, the sticks you and your children will play with will probably be of wood with painted stripes or of brightly colored plastic. The good news is, your fun will not be a bit diminished!

This one is a treasure for rainy days.

SETTING UP

• Your set of sticks will most likely come with values assigned to each stick. If not, assign the values yourself, with the most common sticks having the lowest value, the least common the highest, and the others in between. There are usually two sticks of the highest value that, once freed, can be used as aids to free other sticks.

• For simplicity's sake, you may want to keep the maximum value at ten.

• Players use either a table or the floor.

• The first player holds the sticks in a bunch in one hand just above the surface, then releases them, letting them fall as they may.

HOW TO PLAY

• The first player then tries to extricate sticks, one by one, without moving any other stick in the pile. The player continues to remove sticks until he or she misses, by moving another stick. The next player then takes a turn.

• Once a player has chosen a stick to tackle, he or she may not change and go after another one.

• Each player stockpiles the sticks he or she has accumulated.

WINNING

• Once all the sticks are lifted, the players count points. Whoever has the most number of points (not always the greatest number of sticks) wins.

• There are many interesting techniques to use. More daring players attempt all kinds of flips and flops to extricate their sticks, but in general, this is a quiet and concentrated endeavor.

 GAMES FOR TWO

 **Pease Porridge Hot**

Number of Players: 2
Equipment: None

LORE

Old game books say that this was played by girls in the school-yard to warm their hands on cold mornings. You've probably played it with your infant or toddler as you would Pat-A-Cake. Boys and girls seem to love this game equally at younger ages, but it becomes more the girls' province after toddlerhood.

Not until around age four, when hand-eye coordination really began to sparkle, did we rediscover the challenge of Pease Porridge Hot in our family. See how fast you can get before dissolving with laughter, then watch two young friends, silliness permitted, have a great time. A good waiting game.

HOW TO PLAY
• Players face each other and chant the rhyme that follows.
• As they chant, they alternate clapping their own hands together with clapping their right hands together, own hands together, left hands together, then their own hands together again. There are numerous variations in the method of clapping, and older girls can get quite intricate patterns going. Whether you clap once, twice, double-handed, or double-time, however, just be sure both parties agree on the pattern in the beginning because, after the clap and chant are established ...
• The object of the game is to get faster and faster until one or both parties collapse—usually laughing.

> Pease Porridge hot,
> Pease Porridge cold,
> Pease Porridge in the pot
> Nine days old.
>
> Some like it hot,
> Some like it cold,
> Some like it in the pot
> Nine days old.

Variations
• Here are some other rhymes that adapt well to being clapped:

> My father went to war, war, war
> In Nineteen eighty-four, four, four.
>
> He brought me back a gun, gun, gun
> And it went—BANG!

(At the last line, the first one to say BANG! gets to say the rhyme again while tickling the loser's arm. The loser shouldn't laugh, of course.)

Miss Mary Mack, Mack, Mack
All dressed in black, black, black.
With silver buttons, buttons, buttons
All down her back, back, back.

She asked her Mother, Mother, Mother
For fifty cents, cents, cents
To see the elephant, elephant, elephant
Jump over the fence, fence, fence.

It jumped so high, high, high
It reached the sky, sky, sky.
And never came back, back, back
Till the Fourth of July, ly, LIE!

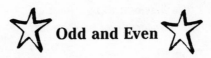 Odd and Even

Number of Players: 2
Equipment: None

LORE
A scene in an Egyptian tomb depicts the playing of a game that apparently used the show of fingers by opposing players, which dates this type of game back at least two thousand years. More recently, if you consider A.D. 60 recent, there exists a description of two shepherds agreeing to play "best of three" to determine which of them would sing first in a contest. The age and worldwide distribution of this game are remarkable—enough to make one appreciate what reliable amusement even little hands hold.

SETTING UP
• The players face each other, one hand of each forming a fist.
• One player chooses to be "Odds," the other "Evens."

HOW TO PLAY
• The players, counting together, extend and withdraw their fists saying "One, two, three, shoot!" then show either their index finger or first two fingers extended to form a V.

WINNING
• If players show the same sign the sum will be even, so the player who has chosen "Evens" wins the round. If players show different signs, the result will be odd, so the player who has chosen "Odds" wins.
• This game is usually played best two out of three, three out of five, and so on, until players are bored.

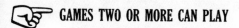 GAMES TWO OR MORE CAN PLAY

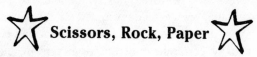 **Scissors, Rock, Paper**

Number of Players: 2–3
Equipment: None

LORE
This ancient game of chance is striking in its simplicity yet provides just enough anticipation to keep children interested from one round to the next. A perfect distraction when waiting on lines, or in between other activities.

SETTING UP
• Different positions of the hand represent three symbols:
Scissors: Extend the index and middle fingers from a fist to make a V shape.
Rock: Make a fist.
Paper: Open the hand, palm down.

HOW TO PLAY
• All players hide a hand behind their back and make one of the symbols. At the count of three, players show their hands.
Scissors can cut paper but is crushed by rock.
Rock crushes scissors but is covered by paper.
Paper covers rock but is cut by scissors.

WINNING
• Each action is usually carried out symbolically by the hands of each player, thus a winner is determined for the round.
• When players present the same symbol, the round is a tie.
• Players usually continue until boredom sets in, but in some instances will play the best two out of three, three out of five, and so on.

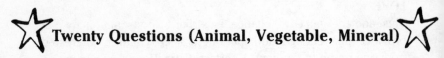

Twenty Questions (Animal, Vegetable, Mineral)

Number of Players: 2 or more
Equipment: None

LORE
This obviously great teaching game is also a world of fun. If it doesn't send you to the encyclopedia regularly, your grammar school education was better than mine!

SETTING UP
It may be necessary to define terms before you begin.

Animal: Any living thing with the exception of the plant world (which is, of course, considered Vegetable) including people, animals, insects, fish, and the like. This category may also include products made from animals such as leather or wool, or milk or eggs, depending on the age and sophistication of players.

Vegetable: Any plant, tree, bush, lichen, bulb, or other "vegetable" matter you can come up with. Again, depending on the sophistication of players, the category may also include any plant product such as cotton, tobacco, or rubber.

Mineral: Any solid inorganic substance that is found in nature or, more simply, anything that is neither animal nor vegetable. Examples are quartz or gold, but minerals can be said to include substances made from organic matter, such as a diamond, or the substances found in foodstuffs. A scientific definition of minerals for you sticklers would include water and mercury.

HOW TO PLAY
• The player who is "It" begins the game by letting the other players know which category contains what he or she is thinking of. For example: "I am thinking of something that is Vegetable."
• The other players must then take turns asking one question each about the mystery "Vegetable" that must be answerable by "yes" or "no."
• The player who is "It" must keep track of the number of questions asked (repeats don't count). If twenty questions are asked without a correct guess, players are told the answer and someone who has not yet been "It" is chosen for the next round.

WINNING
• If a player guesses the correct answer, he or she is "It" next.

HINT
• Ask questions that are fairly specific, of the "Is it bigger than a breadbox?" variety. Some other helpful questions, depending on the category, might be:

> Is it alive?
> Is it edible?
> Is it manufactured?
> Can it be seen in the zoo?

Variation

• Because we use this game as a standard when traveling by car, we tend to let the imagination roam, but the source of objects can be limited to the immediate surroundings—the room, the yard, whatever is in view. You may want to try it each way.

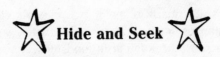 **Hide and Seek**

Number of Players: 2 or more
Equipment: None

LORE
You will be *amazed* at how much children love this game. It's wonderful for a rainy-day-around-the-house, especially with your younger one (it's like a grown-up version of Peek-A-Boo). This game may even have been a rainy-day-around-the-house game in the second century. Records from that time describe a game much like Hide and Seek that is played around the world today. Hide and Seek (also called I Spy, but not to be confused with the other I Spy game described on p. 47) is at its best, however, when played outdoors.

SETTING UP
• A likely spot (tree, bench) is chosen as "home base."
• One player is chosen to be "It."

HOW TO PLAY
• "It" stays at home base, closes his or her eyes, and usually counts to 100. (If the hiding area is small, "It" could count by fives, or count to a lower number agreed upon before play begins.)
• After reaching 100, "It" shouts "Ready or not, here I come," and sets off to find the hiding players.
• When "It" catches sight of a player, he or she runs to touch home base, saying something like "One, two, three, I see Ashley behind the tree."

WINNING
• If the hider can reach the tree first and say "Home free," he or she is "safe."

• The round ends when all players are either caught or safe.
• The first one caught is "It" for the next round.

Variation

SARDINES
Here is a variation of Hide and Seek that turns the tables. Watch the fun when the hiding place turns out to be too small!

HOW TO PLAY
• One player is "It."
• "It" hides while everyone else counts to 100.
• When the players finish counting, they shout "Ready or not, here we come." Everyone then separates and hunts for "It."
• As each player finds "It," he or she very quietly joins "It" in hiding.
• The round is over when the last player finds the hiding place.
• The first player to find "It" becomes "It" for the next round.

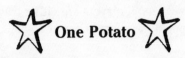 **One Potato**

Number of Players: 2 and up
Equipment: None

LORE
Used as both a game and as a way of determining who is to be "It" in a game, One Potato has never flagged in popularity throughout the twentieth century. You may even remember the call "Spuds Up" to announce a game in your neighborhood.

SETTING UP
• Players gather in a circle, make fists, and hold them out in front with thumb-side up.
• Players agree on a "counter."
• The counter usually begins counting with the player on his or her left but may begin with him- or herself.

HOW TO PLAY
• The counter uses either fist. While saying the rhyme, he or she touches it to each child's fist (potato) in turn around the circle. When the player's own "counting" fist is reached, the player touches it to forehead, eye, nose, or chin.
• The fist touched on the word "more" is "out" and placed behind the player's back.
• The person belonging to the last remaining fist is either "It" or the loser.

> One potato, two potato,
> Three potato, four
> Five potato, six potato
> Seven potato, more.

Tag

Number of Players: 2 or more
Equipment: None

LORE

In the days when objects made of iron were as numerous as objects made of plastic are today, there was a game called Iron Tag, in which players were safe as long as they touched something made of iron. Today, though variations of the game abound, simple Tag is still one of the best-loved and most exciting games of childhood.

SETTING UP

• One player is "It."
• Establish a "home base" and boundaries beyond which players may not go.

HOW TO PLAY

• "It" tries to catch other players by tapping or tagging them as they try to avoid being tagged.
• Players may touch home base for safety once in a while, but they mustn't stay too close or they're likely to hear "Home sticker, lollipop licker!" or a similar chant.
• Once "It" tags someone, that person must then become "It." The game continues until everyone is flushed, thirsty, and—we hope—ready for a nap!

Variations

ARM'S-LENGTH TAG

• This is for two players. One player is "It."

• The players face each other, just far enough apart so that they can barely touch when stretching.

• "It" tries to tag the other player, who tries to avoid being tagged by bending, ducking, turning—anything but moving his or her feet. Good for the younger ones. Fun to do on a bed!

SQUAT TAG

• In lieu of establishing a safe base, players may opt for a number of safe "squats" (usually three) to avoid capture.

• My daughter recently brought home yet another version, TV Tag, in which players must squat and name a television program before being tagged. For me, it's a little too close to "Plastic Tag." I'm hoping to encourage "Book Tag" as an alternative.

FREEZE TAG

• When "It" tags a player, that player must "freeze" where he or she is. A player can be freed by being touched by another player.

• The game is over once "It" is able to "freeze" all the players. The first player frozen is "It" for the next game.

LORE
Hide and Seek is sometimes referred to as I Spy, but we know it also as a different game, one that is tailor-made either for walks or for when one is confined to one room for a period of time.

HOW TO PLAY
• One player surveys the scene and decides on an object in plain view. He or she then gives the only clue: "I spy with my little eye, something that begins with the letter ___."
• The other players take turns guessing what it is that the first player has chosen.

WINNING
• The first player to guess what the object is chooses the next object to be guessed.

Variations
• For younger children, or simply to add variety, a color, shape, or any other defining quality may be used as the clue.

☆ **Dots and Squares** ☆

Number of Players: 2–3
Equipment: Paper, pencils

LORE
LIke Tic-Tac-Toe, Pickup Sticks, and Hangman, this game is a reliable source of enjoyment that is *quiet*—or at least starts out that way. It's also a good way to take a short break with your child when neither of you feels like reading a book.

SETTING UP
• On a blank sheet of paper, draw a horizontal line of six dots, approximately one inch apart. One inch below this row draw another line of six dots, making certain each dot is directly underneath the one above it. Continue in the same manner until there are six rows of dots. It should look like this:

```
•     •     •     •     •     •

•     •     •     •     •     •

•     •     •     •     •     •

•     •     •     •     •     •

•     •     •     •     •     •

•     •     •     •     •     •
```

HOW TO PLAY
• The first player makes a straight line, either horizontal or vertical, connecting two adjacent dots.

• The next player does the same, as does the third, and so on.
• Eventually it will be possible for a player to make a square by drawing the line connecting the last open side. That player then puts his or her initial in the square, and that square becomes the player's. For each completed square, the player gets another turn.
• Each player tries to make as many squares as possible, while avoiding helping the other player(s) complete squares.
• Play continues until all possible squares are made.

WINNING
• The player with the most squares wins.

HINT
• It's a good idea to have different-colored pencils, pens, or markers to make distinguishing squares easier.

Variation

• The game works well with a pyramid and triangles too. Set it up like this:

• In this version lines are made diagonally as well as horizontally and vertically. Have fun!

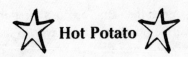 Hot Potato

Number of Players: 2 to many
Equipment: "Potato"

LORE
It's doubtful that you and yours will actually play this game with a potato as they did in the old days—hot or not—but it is good fun with a ball, beanbag, or with any other smallish, soft toy or object.

SETTING UP
• Players form a circle, either standing or sitting.

HOW TO PLAY
• The "Hot Potato" is passed from player to player as quickly as possible.
• Any player to drop the "potato" is out.

WINNING
• The last person left wins.

Variation
• As in Musical Chairs, there is a source of music.
• The "Hot Potato" is passed as quickly as possible from player to player while the music is playing.
• The person holding the "potato" when the music stops is out.

GAMES FOR MORE THAN TWO

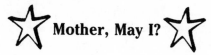 **Mother, May I?**

Number of Players: 3 to many
Equipment: None

LORE

Isn't it amazing how quaint this game sounds? I mean, when was the last time you heard "May I?" from *your* child? Personally, I'm in favor of giving this game an extra boost for its lesson in manners alone, but it also happens to be great fun to play, etiquette aside.

SETTING UP

• One player is "Mother." (Boys may or may not prefer to be "Father" instead.) He or she stands facing the other players, who are in a horizontal line, as far from them as either the room will allow or, if outdoors, perhaps twenty feet distant. Players should stand an arm's length or more apart from each other.

• There are four basic kinds of "step" players can take in this game, but please feel free to add your own:

   Baby step: The smallest step, accomplished by putting the heel of one foot directly in front of the toe of the other.

   Regular step: Exactly that, one normal walking stride.

   Umbrella step: Accomplished by walking and turning at the same time.

   Giant step: The longest step a player can manage.

HOW TO PLAY

• "Mother" addresses each player in turn, telling him or her how many of which kind of step to take.

• Before a player can move, however, he or she must say "Mother, may I?" and wait for a reply. Mother can either say "Yes, you may," or she can be capricious, as all mothers are, and say "No, you may not," and substitute another step or combination of steps, either forward or backward.

• The players, of course, are all trying their best to maximize the distance of the steps they take because the object of the game is to get close enough to Mother to sneak up and tag her while her attention is elsewhere and she cannot protest. In order to achieve this end, players may also try to sneak in steps when Mother isn't looking. If they're caught, however, they must go back to the starting line.

• Mother in the meantime tries to keep everyone at bay for as long as possible. Sounds a lot like motherhood to me.

WINNING

• The first player to tag Mother, gets to be Mother next.

• It's not fair for Mother to take to the high ground and not let the other players have a sporting chance at her. Mother, May I? is not for the timid!

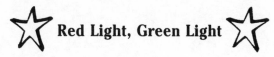

Red Light, Green Light

Number of Players: 3 to many
Equipment: None

LORE

This game is similar in set-up and principle to Mother, May I? but differs enough to warrant its own description.

SETTING UP

• One player is the "Police Officer." He or she stands facing other players, who are in a horizontal line. The Officer is as far away from other players as either room will allow or, if outdoors, perhaps twenty feet distant.

• The Officer turns his or her back to other players, says "Green light," and counts out loud to five as quickly as possible. The other players can walk or run toward the Officer as quickly as possible while his or her back is still turned.

• The Officer then says "Red light" and whirls to face the other players. If the Officer catches anyone moving, that person is out for the remainder of the round or must return to the starting line.

• Each player tries to be the first to tag the Officer while his or her back is still turned.

WINNING

• The first player to accomplish this is the Officer for the next round.

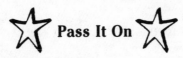 **Pass It On**

Number of Players: 3 or more
Equipment: None

LORE
This informal game may not have the provenance of some of the others in this book, but I'm a fan because it seems a great precursor to the noble game of Charades, which I was always too shy to play. Four- to six-year-olds, however, seem to take to this game with great relish. Who knows, they may turn into Charades players when they're older.

HOW TO PLAY
• Players form a row.
• The first child in line thinks of an object, then pretends to lift it and pass it to the next person in line. It can be heavy or light, large or small, or even alive! If it's a box, it must be a box containing something specific; if it has shape, the shape should be apparent in the way it's held.
• The second child in line receives the object and tries to pass it along the same way.
• This must all be done in pantomime, of course.
• When the last child in line receives the object, he or she tries to guess what it is.
• If that player cannot guess, the others can guess in turn. If everyone gives up, the first player must tell what the object was.
• After the object is known, the first player goes to the end of the line and a new game begins.

Red Rover

Number of Players: The more the better
Equipment: None

LORE
Long known as a popular street game, Red Rover is now played in fields and gymnasiums as well. It's very lively and exciting.

SETTING UP
• Players will need a fair amount of space. Teams should not stand directly in front of walls or other obstructions.
• Two teams are formed. The teams stand approximately twelve feet apart, facing each other. Team members either hold hands or link arms.

HOW TO PLAY
• Teams take turns calling players over. When a person is agreed upon, the team rocks back and forth chanting "Red Rover, Red Rover, let _____ come over!"
• When that player hears his or her name, he or she runs at the opposition and tries to break through the line.
• If the player is successful, he or she may go back to his or her own team. If the player does not succeed in breaking through, he or she must join the other team.

WINNING
• When all the players are on one team, the game is over. However, as this happens only rarely (and would take forever), you may want to set a time limit and designate the team that ends up with the most members the winner.

Variation #1

• An actual "Red Rover" may be chosen to stand between the two teams and call out the names of players, who must then run to the other side and try to break the human chain. This avoids delays and arguments among teammates who want to call different people over.
• In this version, when a player is unsuccessful, he or she must take the place of Red Rover, who rejoins the play on the opposing team.

Variation #2

• All players line up on one side, with "Red Rover" on the other.
• Colors, rather than names, are called. Anyone wearing the color called must cross the space between where the players are standing and where Red Rover stands without being caught. Any player who is caught helps Red Rover catch more people.
• The game ends when everyone is on the same side.

Johnny, May We Cross Your River?

Number of Players: The more the better
Equipment: None

LORE

This game is of the same ilk as Red Rover, but not as closely associated with the city streets. Perhaps it was the country folks' version of a super game for large groups, requiring space to run and screaming room too.

SETTING UP

• A "safe zone" is established at each end of the playing area. A total space of about twenty-five feet is ideal.

• "Johnny" stands on one safety line, the other players line up on the other, facing Johnny.

• Players ask as a group, "Johnny, may we cross your river?"

• Johnny answers, "Not unless you ... (wear the color black, have red hair, are missing two front teeth, and so on).

• Players who qualify get free passage to safety "across the river"; other players may try to bluff their way across, make a run for it, or wait for the next answer to see if they have the necessary requirement.

• Amid all this turmoil Johnny has to try to catch the wily player who tries to sneak across undetected or the brazen one who bolts across. If Johnny does, that player becomes Johnny and the old Johnny joins the group of players who haven't yet crossed over.

• When all players are on the same side of the "river" as Johnny, then Johnny joins them himself, another Johnny is chosen, and play continues.

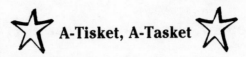

A-Tisket, A-Tasket

Number of Players: 5 or more
Equipment: Handkerchief

LORE
In Victorian times this game was known as a kissing game that was played at country fairs. (Don't tell your children.) In all probability, it had its beginning long before as a fertility rite. (Definitely don't tell your children.)

SETTING UP
• One player is "It." He or she holds the handkerchief.
• The other players hold hands and form a circle, with "It" on the outside.

HOW TO PLAY
• "It" skips around the circle singing the rhyme.
• On the last words, "It" drops the handkerchief behind a player and continues to skip around the circle. The other player must pick the handkerchief up and skip around the circle the other way in order to get back to his or her place.

WINNING
• Whichever player arrives at the empty place first joins the circle, and the other must be "It" for the next round.

> A-Tisket, A-Tasket,
> A green and yellow basket
>
> I wrote a letter to my love
> And on the way I dropped it

I dropped it, I dropped it
And on the way I dropped it

Somebody here has picked it up
And put it in your pocket;
It isn't you, it isn't you—
It's you!

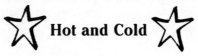 **Hot and Cold**

Number of Players: 4–6 ideal
Equipment: Small object

LORE

Hot and Cold is probably a relative of that Victorian classic Hunt the Thimble, which also turned into Huckle Buckle Jelly Bean. Hot and Cold, however, lets more people in on the joke, and invariably leads to much excitement, screaming, and shrieking.

SETTING UP

• The small object to be hidden is shown to all the players.
• One player is "It." Players determine the sequence of players who will be "It."
• The other players agree on a hiding place for the object.

HOW TO PLAY

• Players hide the object while "It" is out of the room (or, if play is outdoors, where he or she can't see).
• Players then sit or stand in a group and call "It" back into the room.
• "It" tries to find the hidden object.

• If "It" is nowhere near the hidden object, players call "Cold." If "It" is in the general vicinity of the object, players call "Warm." And if "It" is close or very close to the object, players call "Hot" until the object is found.

• Next "It" leaves the room, and play begins as before.

WINNING
• Should you have a particularly competitive group on your hands, you can time each player's search for the object. The player whose time is the shortest wins.

Musical Chairs

Number of Players: 4 or more
Equipment: Chairs or sheets of construction paper for all but one player; source of music that can be turned on and off

LORE
Musical Chairs is the classic birthday party game, along with Pin the Tail on the Donkey. Musical Chairs, however, takes very little preparation when there are four or more children around the house. It's also a good way for them to let off a little steam without bouncing off the walls.

SETTING UP
• Count the number of players, then set chairs for all but one player either in two rows back to back or in a circle, facing outward. (Should you have many players and few chairs, tape sheets of construction paper to the floor about a foot apart.)
• The music source should be supervised by an adult to prevent breakage, screaming, arguments, and the like.
• Players arrange themselves more or less in front of chairs.

HOW TO PLAY
• When the music begins, players walk around chairs and continue walking until the music stops.
• As soon as the music stops, each player must sit down in a chair (or stand on a piece of paper). As there is one less chair than players, someone will be caught unseated. That person steps out. (Depending on the music source and your daring, the person who is just out can control the next round of music.)
• Take away one chair at the beginning of each new round.

WINNING
• At some point there will be two eager little bodies circling one chair. Whoever prevails wins.

3

. . . .

Classic Games for Ages Six to Eight

Along with many of the physical games introduced from ages four to six, which will serve your child well for many years to come, between the ages of six and eight a new element begins to make itself apparent—sophistication. Not only will your child be capable of much greater dexterity and coordination, but he or she will pursue these challenges avidly. Your child will be responsive to games with rules having a fair degree of complexity and will take pride in mastering a number of different activities. Children at this age will often go back to games they have played in the past and "really get them right."

Don't think, however, that your child will turn quietly intellectual. He or she is just as likely to bruise a knee or bloody a lip on the playground—but perhaps in a more organized fashion.

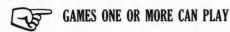 **GAMES ONE OR MORE CAN PLAY**

⭐ Concentration (or Memory) ⭐

Number of Players: 1–4
Equipment: Playing cards

LORE
Card games in general are centuries old and have always been well loved and much played. This one is particularly good since it is versatile enough to be satisfying whether played by one or, with added decks, by many.

SETTING UP
• For the less-experienced player cards are set out in rows, face-down, within reach of all players. For players with more experience, cards are set out helter-skelter, facedown, within reach of all players.

HOW TO PLAY
• The first player chooses two cards to turn face up. If these match—that is, are of the same value—the player gets to keep the cards and try again until he or she turns up two cards that do not match. All players must be able to see the cards.
• If only one child is playing, he or she continues to overturn cards two by two until all pairs are matched. To further the challenge, he or she may play against a clock or against him- or herself.
• If there are more than two players, turns continue in a clockwise direction.

WINNING
• The player with the most pairs at the end of the game wins.

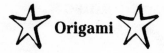 Origami

Number of Players: 1 or more
Equipment: Supple paper, patterned or colored

LORE

Origami isn't actually a game, it's the ancient and esteemed Japanese art of folding paper. Long ago, origami figures were so complex and costly that they were used only for special or ceremonial occasions and their creation required the skill of an expert. A custom called the *noshi*, dating back to the twelfth century, however, aided the evolution of origami into an everyday part of Japanese life. A *noshi* is a folded paper ornament containing a strip of dried abalone, which was traditionally attached to gifts. It represented the wish of the giver that the recipient enjoy good fortune. The making of the *noshi* became the enjoyable task of Japanese housewives, who have taught their children the art of paper folding for amusement as well as tradition for many years.

Though the practice of origami can get incredibly intricate and exquisite, learning to make a paper airplane, and a simple sailboat, and in the next section, a Fortune Teller, will be sufficient introduction for those who want to embark on this increasingly popular craft. For those who don't, you will still have mastered the ability to create three of childhood's indispensable playthings.

SAILBOAT

1. Life immediately becomes easier once you learn how to make a square piece of paper from a rectangular one. Hold the rectangle in front of you with long sides at top and bottom. Take the upper left-hand corner of the paper and bring it down to the lower left-hand corner. Now slide the upper corner along the bottom edge of the paper toward the right-hand side of the paper until it forms a perfect triangle. Make a deep crease in the paper to keep the triangle. You will have a rectangular flap "left over" on the right-hand side of the paper. Fold this either over or under the edge of the triangle, and tear it off. Open your triangle and—voilà!—you now have a square. It's easy once you've done it—I promise.

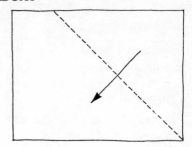

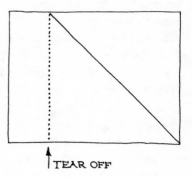

TEAR OFF

2. Take your square, which has one corner-to-corner fold in it, unfold it, and make a sharp crease from the other corner-to-corner diagonal, on the same side. Then unfold it and turn it over.

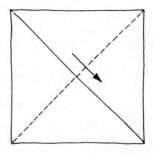

3. Now fold the paper in half so that it opens up like a book. Remember to make your creases sharp and strong.

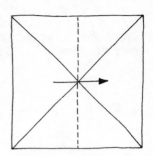

4. Fold it like a book the other way. Leave it folded.

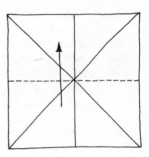

5. Here is where your strong creases will help you. Take the ends of the folded paper and push them toward each other until the upper four corners of the paper meet. You may have to jiggle them around a little, but it does happen. Press flat. You will now have a diamond shape, with flaps front and back and folds on the sides.

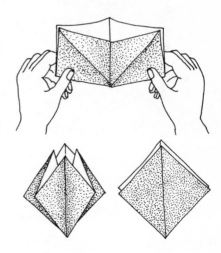

6. Open your paper into a large diamond. Bring the top and bottom corners to the center fold. Crease and hold down.

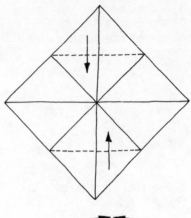

7. Bring two large points to meet each other, using the folds you've already made. Press flat. Now you can see it taking shape.

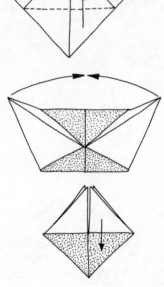

8. Fold one "sail" down over the front of the "boat." Fold the sail back up, but leave a small pleat at the base of the sail so it becomes shorter than the other. Tuck pleat into the boat. Turn the boat over.

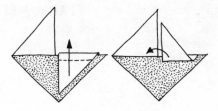

9. Fold the bottom point of the boat up to make a base on which the boat will stand.
• Time to go sailing!

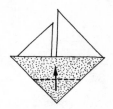

PAPER AIRPLANE

1. Fold a rectangle of paper (typing paper is fine) in half lengthwise. Crease hard.

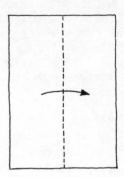

2. Fold bottom corners to the center line. Crease hard.

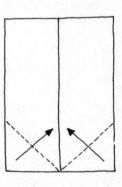

3. Fold each of the flaps you've just made in half. The point should get pointier, the new flaps should meet at the center line.

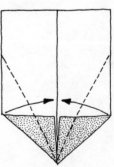

4. Do the same thing once more. The folds always meet at the center line.

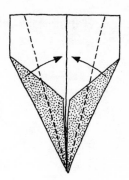

5. Fold your airplane in half lengthwise, folding sides down and away from you.

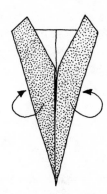

6. That's it! Spread the "wings" and hold the center fold together from underneath with thumb and forefinger. Pull back and let 'er go! (See illustration.)

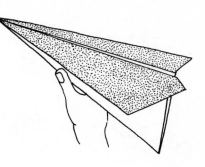

☞ **GAMES TWO OR MORE CAN PLAY**

☆ **Fortune Teller** ☆

Number of Players: 2 and up
Equipment: Paper, paints, markers, or crayons

SETTING UP
The making of a Fortune Teller can be as much fun as playing the game itself—and usually takes longer! The combination of coloring, craft, imagination, and play makes it a powerful contender in the world of games. In fact, it seems to be a prime obsession of young girls.

1. Make your square sheet of paper once more. (See "sailboat" p. 66)

1a. Make a crease along the other diagonal—one will already be creased.

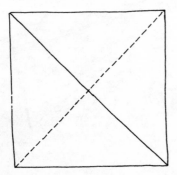

2. Lay the paper flat. Fold each corner into the middle and crease

hard. Your square will now look like a diamond. **2a.**

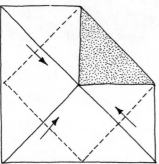

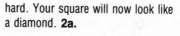
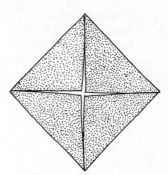

3. Turn the paper over. Once again, fold all corners into the middle. You will have a square again. **3a.**

4. Fold the square in half along the horizontal. You now have a fold along the bottom edge and two "flaps" on either side—a total of four "flaps."

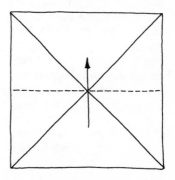

4a. Slide your right thumb under the front right flap. Slide your right forefinger under the rear right flap. Press your thumb and forefinger together to grasp. Slide your left thumb under the front left flap. Slide your left forefinger under the rear left flap. Press your thumb and forefinger together to grasp.

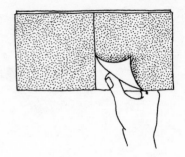

5. As you did with the boat, push until the points at the top meet in the middle. It should look like figure 5. Reinforce all folds. That's it! Now here's how it works:

6. Holding from the bottom once more, push all points together. This is a closed Fortune Teller. Now pull away and you will see a diamond-shaped pocket appear. This is the first open position of the Fortune Teller. Push together again. Press your thumbs together through the paper and your index fingers together through the paper. Separate your thumb and index finger on each hand until you see a diamond-shaped pocket that goes in the opposite direction of the first. This is the second position of the Fortune Teller.

Practice until you can slide back and forth from one position to the other easily. Now comes the creative part.

7. Open the Fortune Teller into the small square it becomes when it is flat. Turn it over. With markers, paints, or crayons, color each of the smaller squares that take up one-quarter of the paper a different color. Then turn it over.

8. On the side with the flaps, number each triangle consecutively from one to eight. You'll notice that when you go from position to po-

sition, four numbers show each time—two odd and two even.
9. Unfold all the flaps, and in the triangles under each number write a fortune, wonderful or funny, ex- aggerated, mysterious, ridiculous, or maybe scary (but not too). Now you are ready to play Fortune Teller. (After you've refolded your paper, of course.)

HOW TO PLAY

• The first player holds the Fortune Teller in a closed position so that only the colors are seen.
• The second player chooses a color.
• The first player opens and closes the Fortune Teller once for every letter in the color chosen, alternating directions so that first one set of numbers show, then the other. The Fortune Teller stays open on the last letter.
• The second player then chooses a number and the Fortune Teller opens and closes as before, stopping (open) when the number is reached.
• The second player chooses a number once more, but this time the first player opens the flap and reads the second player's fortune.
• The second player then gets to work the Fortune Teller for the first player.

HINT

• Much of the amusement (aside from making the Fortune Teller) depends on the fortunes made up—encourage the imagination! Of course, this could lead to the unexpected too. Our daughter was inordinately proud of one of her first efforts and persuaded a somewhat dignified friend of ours to join the fun, which he good-naturedly did. What was his fortune? "You have head lice!" Not one of our finer moments.

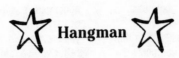

Hangman

Number of Players: 2–4
Equipment: Paper, pencils

LORE
All the grisly and imaginative explanations you or I could think of concerning the origin of this particular quiet and "intellectual" game must, I'm afraid, remain in the realm of speculation for the time being. Though many seem to know how to play it, there doesn't seem to be an easy answer to where it came from—or when. It will just have to remain a mysterious—and well-loved—classic.

SETTING UP
1. The first player thinks of a word of five letters or more, and makes the appropriate number of dashes on a piece of paper along with the gallows for all to see.

HOW TO PLAY
2. The second player guesses a letter of the word. If he or she is right, that letter goes in its proper place on the line of dashes. If the guess is wrong, the first line of the "Hangman" is drawn from the gallows and the incorrect letter is written below the line of dashes so players don't guess the same letter twice.
• If a letter guessed occurs more than once in the word, it must be written in each place it occurs.
• Players continue guessing letters in turn either until the complete Hangman is drawn, or one of the players guesses the word.

WINNING
• If the complete Hangman is drawn with no one guessing the word, the same player gets to choose the next word.

• The player to guess the word first gets to choose the word for the next round.
• Here is what the Hangman looks like:

Variation
• Agreeing on a theme such as sayings, book titles, movies, historical characters—anything you like—can make the game longer, more interesting, more difficult, more fun.

⭐ Hopscotch ⭐

Number of Players: 2 or more
Equipment: Chalk, place marker, flat surface outdoors

LORE
Here is another ancient game, as popular as ever today, so much so that Hopscotch is almost synonymous with childhood and play—to wit, all the movies where characters, to show their light-heartedness, hop through the chalk drawing in a playground, usually to the accompaniment of insipid music. Never mind that, however. Hopscotch has a long and fascinating history and much juicy symbolism to sort out. Here are some highlights.

Hopscotch is as widespread as it is old. Diagrams for the game have been found on the pavement of the old Forum in Rome.

A Spanish children's game of old, *A La Pata Coja*, was played on one foot; the other foot was said to be lame. The word *hop* in Old English actually means "to walk lamely," so it is probable that the German version of Hopscotch, *Hinkespiel*, and Danish, *hinkeleg paradis*, also have to do with hopping around on one foot, pretending to be lame. To neaten the package even more, the word *scotch* derives from "scratch," which means line.

Olden versions of the game apparently had to do with the travels and travails of the soul from earth to heaven. In Norway it was called *paradishopping*. As we all know, no trip to paradise is without its pitfalls, and in Hopscotch these could be avoided by not stepping on the lines, not losing one's balance, or not misthrowing the marker. Some of the dangers include running into witches, crocodiles, poison, snakes, swamps, dragons, bad luck, and bears. The long-ago associations and superstitions connected with stepping on lines, which are still acknowledged today to some extent, include such horrors as losing one's hair, falling down stairs, breaking a teapot, being snakebitten, breaking the Devil's back—or your mother's. Add to that the threat of a bad marriage, and you can imagine many children of old tiptoeing around quite carefully. Should you manage to avoid all of these catastrophes, the goal to be attained was not always heaven or paradise but could be home, an ice-cream cone, or even a radish! As there always are a few intrepid children in this world, lines were sometimes to be stepped on in order to see just what the future might hold.

The "marker" went by many names: tor, lagger, puck, potsy, dump, scotch, pally-ully—you may have a few of your own. Everything imaginable was used; stones, shells, wood, keys, toys, bottlecaps, beanbags, chalk, potsherds, even paper that was blown from square to square.

SETTING UP

1. As you can see, there are a number of ways a Hopscotch game can be set up. What is needed is a level place that can be drawn on with chalk. Draw one of the figures illustrated, with boxes approximately one-and-one-half feet square. Number each box, beginning with 1. Each player has a place marker: a stone, potsherd, or any other small object that can be thrown into the squares. Draw a line a few feet from the bottom of the diagram. The marker must be thrown from behind this line.

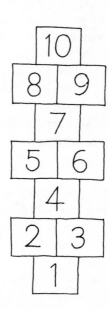

HOW TO PLAY

• The first player stands behind the line and throws his or her marker into square 1.

• The player must hop directly into square 2, then, depending on how the squares are set up, alternate hopping on one foot and jumping into two boxes side by side with one foot in each box.

• When the end is reached, the player in one jump must turn around and repeat the alternate one-and-two-foot hopping and jumping until he or she reaches square 2. The player must then stand on one foot and bend down to retrieve his or her marker, from square 1, then jump out. The player continues by throwing the marker into square 2, and repeats the sequence, avoiding stepping into square 2 both going and coming and also avoiding any square in which a marker has been left by another player.

• A player loses a turn whenever he or she misses the square aimed for with the marker, steps on a line or into any square with a marker in it, or puts two feet down in a single box or at the wrong time.

• For the player who has gotten all the way through the diagram and is about to blow it as he or she is losing balance reaching for the marker, there is one last chance. If the player can say "Butter-fingers" before touching the ground with a hand to regain balance, he or she can then regain composure and try again. If not, however, it's o-u-t.

• When a player misses, he or she deposits the marker in the square to be repeated and leaves it there until his or her next turn.

• If there are too many markers in squares to permit a player to pass, then temporary boxes—"boxies"—can be drawn next to the occupied ones with a broken line.

WINNING

• The player who is first able to complete the journey through the Hopscotch and back is the winner, and should receive his or her just reward—a radish, perhaps?

• If, by some chance, this all seems too easy to you, do it the way the Burmese do: Squat on your heels, hands on hips, and hop from square to square without losing your balance!

Variations
• Rather than picking your marker up on the way back, players might kick it out of the square either coming or going—decide which in advance.
• Domes or other shapes of "rest areas" (in some places referred to as "the Pot") are often drawn at the top of the diagram, but don't linger too long! (See illustration.)

Marbles

Number of Players: 2 and up
Equipment: Chalk, 1 shooter, 8 or 10 marbles per player

LORE

If you can picture a group of cavepeople sitting around playing this game, you may not be too far from wrong. Smooth, round stones much resembling marbles have been discovered along with other relics of prehistory. If that is too much of a leap of the imagination for you, however, the game was certainly popular in ancient Egypt, Greece, and Rome. In Rome at the time of the poet Ovid (43 B.C.–A.D. 18), children rolled nuts down an inclined plane and tried to hit other nuts grouped at the bottom. A similar game was well known in the Middle Ages. A rhyme about marbles much as we know it is recorded in a book that dates back to 1771. Even Abraham Lincoln played marbles. Moreover, marbles has been played with everything from musketballs and cranberries to nuts and crabapples and, of course, rounded bits of marble.

Today there is an incredible amount of mythology and terminology associated with the game of Marbles. A mystique and brotherhood surrounds old Marbles players who reminisce about "spannies" (a handspan used to determine whether a marble is near enough to take another), "steelies" (marbles made from hollow steel), "burnings" (breathing on a marble for luck), and numerous other terms that varied from neighborhood to neighborhood—and sometimes from street to street.

Good for you if you can remember your terminology and have retained your technique, but watch out for your offspring. As you will remember, this can be a bloodthirsty game!

SETTING UP

There are many, many variations of Marbles. What we'll learn here is one way to play a variant called Ringers.

• Draw a circle approximately two feet in diameter on a flat, smooth surface. Now draw another circle of about six feet in diameter around the first circle. Players must always shoot from outside this circle.

• Each player keeps his or her "shooter" (a marble that is larger than the rest) in hand.

• Depending on the number of players, one, two, or three marbles from each player are placed in the center of the ring at the beginning of play. This comprises the "pot."

HOW TO PLAY

• The first player places his or her shooter (also called knuckler) behind the designated line and propels it toward the marbles grouped in the center. The aim is to knock as many marbles as possible out of the inside ring.

• Marbles may be propelled by rolling, throwing, squeezing between two fingers, flicking between thumb and forefinger—or come up with a variation of "knuckling down" of your own!

• The player may "capture" any marbles of opposing players that he or she knocks out of the ring. The catch here is that the shooter marble must stay *inside* the ring in order for the player to capture the marbles knocked out.

• If the player has knocked one or more marbles out of the inside ring and the shooter remains inside, he or she retrieves the shooter and takes another turn. This continues until the player misses.

WINNING
• The player having the most marbles after all are shot from the ring is the winner. Decide in advance whether games are "for keeps" or not.

Variations
• A single circle ten feet in diameter is drawn. Thirteen marbles are placed in a cross in the center of the circle. When two are playing, the first person to knock seven marbles out of the circle wins.
• When a younger sibling has to get into the act, try Bombardier. Draw a circle about two feet in diameter. Put ten marbles in the middle, then stand and drop your shooter into the pile. The one who knocks the most marbles from the ring wins.

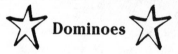

Dominoes

Number of Players: 2–4
Equipment: Set of dominoes

LORE
Dominoes is a simple game popular in many countries throughout the world. The first set of dominoes may have come from China, where they were used in divination, to Europe as early as the fourteenth century. By the eighteenth century they were all the rage in Italy.

Their resemblance to dice is intentional. Twenty-one of the pieces represent the permutations of throwing two dice (each half of the domino stands for one die), with the remaining seven of the standard set of twenty-eight being the blank suit. Old sets were carved of dark woods, ivory, or bone. Modern sets may be painted wood or plastic.

The simplest of domino games, Double Six or Draw, is what we'll learn here.

SETTING UP

Before you actually begin to play, here are some Domino facts and terms you shouldn't leave home without.

• There are seven double dominoes, twenty-one single dominoes.

• A set of dominoes is called a **deck**.

• The dominoes a player chooses is called a **hand**.

• Choosing your dominoes is called **drawing a hand**.

• The pile of dominoes left after hands are chosen is called the **boneyard**—can you guess why?

• To get rid of all your dominoes is **to domino**.

Now, here's how to begin:

• On a tabletop or other flat surface, turn all dominoes facedown and mix them up.

• If two are playing, each player takes seven dominoes. If three or more play, each player takes five dominoes and sets them in front of him or her so that the other players cannot see them. The remaining dominoes become the boneyard, from which players may draw when necessary. Move the boneyard out of the center but within easy reach of all players.

HOW TO PLAY

• Players determine who has the highest double (matching ends). That player begins by placing the domino in the center of the table. Turns proceed clockwise. If no player has a double, dominoes are returned to the pile, mixed again, and redrawn.

• The second player must match an end of one of his or her

dominoes to the double. He or she places the matching end perpendicular to the double, at its center. Only the side of the double may be played, not the ends.

• The third player may match either the other side of the original double in the same way as did the second player, or the free end of the second player's domino. Dominoes, unless they are doubles, are placed lengthwise end to end, with ends matching. Doubles are always placed across the line of play.

• Blanks are matched to blanks, unless they are specified "wild" at the beginning of the game, in which case they can be anything.

• One domino is played per turn.

• If a player is unable to match the open end of any row, he or she draws from the boneyard until a match can be made.

• Dominoes may be played in any direction or pattern in order to prevent them from falling off the playing surface.

• If the last domino is taken from the boneyard and a player still cannot play, he or she misses a turn and play continues.

• If possible, players must play a domino. The object of the game is to get rid of all your dominoes.

• If the wrong (that is, not matching) domino is played and is not noticed until after the next domino is played, the wrong domino is treated as if it were the right domino, and play continues. If it is noticed before the next turn, however, it must be removed, so watch out for bluffers!

WINNING

• The player who uses all of his or her dominoes first wins the round. He or she counts the number of dots on opponents' remaining dominoes, which is his or her score for the round.

• If the round must end because no one can play a domino, the player with the fewest dots wins the round. Opponents' dots are counted, but the winning player must subtract the number of his or her remaining dots from the score.

• First player to reach 100 points wins the game.

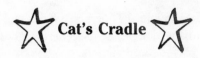

Cat's Cradle

Number of Players: 2
Equipment: Thick string about 3 feet long, ends tied together

LORE

This fascinating, hypnotic, and skillful game of weaving designs in string on the fingers came to us from long ago. Primitive cultures around the world made designs in string for pleasure, artistic expression, and often as an aid to storytelling. Certain tribes of Eskimos known for their artistic accomplishments created some of the world's most beautiful and complex string figures. Young Eskimo boys, however, were not allowed to learn string weaving because their elders feared their fingers would tangle the harpoon lines during the hunt. In the seventeenth century, string games were probably learned in Asia by tea traders, who then brought them back to Europe and England. By 1782 English children had appropriated the games. Charles Lamb, the English essayist (1775–1834), was among those who remember weaving Cat's Cradles as a schoolboy.

SETTING UP

You can learn many variations for this game, and the names of figures vary greatly from place to place. Although what we have here is a basic starter set of games, if you've never made Cat's Cradles before it will be a challenge! If it all begins to look too complicated, just remember the fundamental movement: picking up *X*'s over, under, or in between the straight strings. (See the illustration.)

CAT'S CRADLE

1. The first player places a loop of string around the backs of the fingers (not thumbs) of each hand.

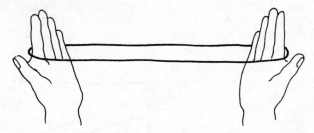

2. The player brings his or her hands together, puts the right hand under the front string, and pulls back. There should be a loop around the right hand. Then he or she brings the hands together again. This time the player puts the left hand under the front string and pulls back. There should now be a loop around the left hand too.

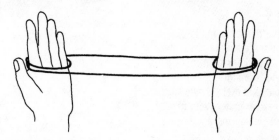

3. The player brings the hands together, picks the string that crosses the left palm up with the right middle finger, and pulls back. Then he or she brings the hands together again. The player picks the string that crosses the right palm up with the left middle finger and pulls back. This is the basic Cat's Cradle.

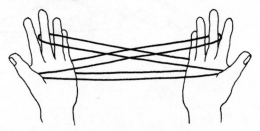

DIAMONDS

From Cat's Cradle position, the partner pinches the *X*'s on each side of the cradle between thumb and forefinger. He or she pulls them out past the side strings, then goes under and comes up again between them, taking the figure from the partner. When the player separates thumbs and forefingers and pulls the hands apart, there will be a diamond in the middle.

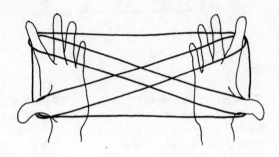

PINKIES

1. The partner takes the long *X*'s that make the diamond shape in center and pinches them between thumb and forefinger. He or she lifts up, out, and over the side strings, then comes up under them toward the center, taking the figure from the partner's hands.

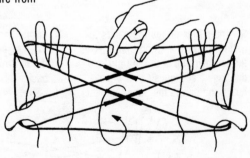

2. When the player separates thumb
and forefinger and pulls the hands
apart, there will be one long loop on
either side of the figure.

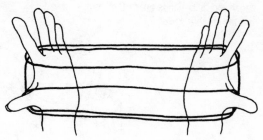

DOUBLE *X*'s

1. Using the pinkies, the partner
takes the right middle string with
the left pinkie and the left middle
string with the right pinkie. He
pulls the right pinkie over the left,
the left goes under the right, and
holds tightly. Then he or she pulls
the pinkies out to the side past the
end strings, and pulls down and
holds. Now he or she takes the
thumb and forefinger, places them
close together, and puts them
down through the small triangles
formed at the sides of the figure.

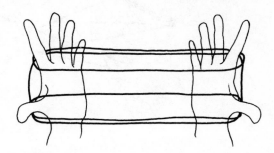

2. The thumb and forefinger come up again with the side strings on the outside of the hands. Then the player separates thumb and forefinger and pulls hands apart. Can you see the double X's?

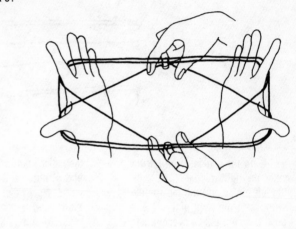

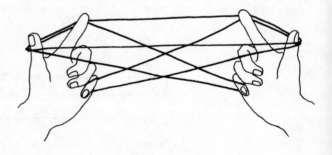

BRIDGES

The partner takes the *X*'s formed on the side of the figure between the thumb and forefinger. He or she pulls out, over, and down through the middle, taking the figure from the partner. Hands will be palm down. He or she spreads the fingers. Bridges turns to Diamonds, but with hands palm downward.

• To keep going, keep pinching *X*'s and pulling over or under side strings.

• To stop—let go!

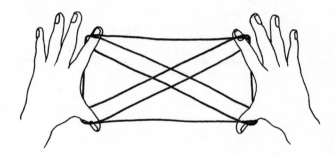

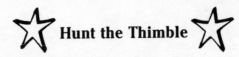 **Hunt the Thimble**

Number of Players: 2 or more
Equipment: Thimble, jellybean, or other small object

LORE
Here is an old Victorian parlor game that probably originated with a harassed mother who had—what else—lost her thimble. In our house it could be called "Where are my glasses?" Whatever its origin, however, or its variations, it's a winner on a rainy day, and a special treat if the "object" is edible.

SETTING UP
• One player is "It."
• While other players are out of the room, "It" places a thimble within a designated area in plain sight, but in a spot that might be easily overlooked.

HOW TO PLAY
• Players return to the room when "It" is ready, and try to find the thimble without disturbing anything in the room.
• If a player spots it, he or she must—without saying anything and without looking at it—sit down and wait for the rest of the players to find it.

WINNING
• The first player to see the thimble gets to hide it in the next round.

 **GAMES FOR MORE THAN TWO**

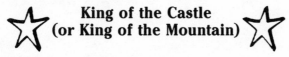

King of the Castle
(or King of the Mountain)

Number of Players: 3 or more
Equipment: None

LORE
Being one of the simplest games to play, and the most easily understood, it's no surprise that this one is a very ancient game. Horace, writing in 20 B.C., quoted the rhyme as we understand it, and in eighteenth-century England it was known as "Keep the Castle." A great game for the beach.

SETTING UP
• Players must find or construct a mound (something soft, please) atop which only one person may stand at a time.

HOW TO PLAY
• One person is chosen King. He or she stands on the mound and dares all comers to push him or her off.
• The player who succeeds in getting the King off the castle then takes his or her place. If two or more are responsible the matter can be settled by Odds and Evens.
• Players must not use excessive force, pull on clothing, or do anything other than push or pull the King.

WINNING
• A fleeting and temporary occurrence. The winner is the King able to keep "the rascals" at bay. Players may want to set an actual time limit—say three minutes.

> I'm the King of the Castle,
> Get down, you dirty Rascal!

Statues

Number of Players: 5 or more
Equipment: None

LORE

Statues is a good lawn game as it needs space without obstruction. It's also a good game for a mixed-age group as it doesn't depend on competitive physical skills, such as running, or on verbal abilities. As a matter of fact, in the Victorian era it was a slightly different game, geared to an older crowd. Couples would dance around the room to music, which would be stopped (much as in Musical Chairs). The dancing couples then froze where they were until the music started again. Anyone who moved was out. The last couple left won. Statues may not date back to ancient times, but a number of generations have enjoyed it already, and it looks as if it's well on its way to becoming a documented classic.

Because it is so antic and animated, and great for spontaneous innovation and amusement, this one may tempt you to join in yourself—even without music!

SETTING UP

• One player is the Statue Maker.
• Before each child is swung, the Statue Maker asks whether he or she wants a slow (salt), medium (sugar), or fast (pepper) swing.

HOW TO PLAY

• The Statue Maker and a player extend their arms and clasp hands as if for a handshake. The Statue Maker then swings the player around three times.

• Just before letting the player go, the Statue Maker tells the player what to be: funny, sad, sleepy, scary; or something specific—a kangaroo, a cartoon character, a rosebush, a person they both know; or even an object—a sack of potatoes, a motorcycle, a book. The wilder the request, the more fun the game.

• The player is let go and tumbles through space, freezing in whatever position he or she happens to land (of course also trying to arrange it so he or she "just happens" to freeze in a posture resembling the Statue Maker's request).

• The Statue Maker repeats this process with the remaining players.

• The Statue Maker then chooses the player judged to be the best, and that player becomes the next Statue Maker.

• If a player is unable to maintain the frozen position, he or she is disqualified from that round. This often happens when someone collapses with laughter.

Buzz

Number of Players: 3 or more
Equipment: None

LORE
This is a game sure to test your wits as well as your child's. We play it on trips in the car—but not for too long!

SETTING UP
• Players determine the order in which they will go.
• The word "Buzz" is substituted for the number seven, any number containing a seven, or any multiple of seven. For example, seven would be "Buzz," seventy would be "Buzz-ty," but twenty-one is plain "Buzz."

HOW TO PLAY
• The first player says "One," second player says "Two" and so on until seven is reached, which must be "Buzz." Thereafter, "Buzz" must be substituted as described, with players counting as fast as they can.
• Any player who misses is out.

WINNING
• The last player left wins.

Variations

BUZZ-FIZZ
• If you really want to drive yourself and/or your children crazy, substitute the word "Fizz" for the number five, any number con-

taining five, or any multiple of five, at the same time you are substituting "Buzz" for seven. In the case of thirty-five, for example, you have a "Buzz-Fizz," where at fifty-seven you must say,"Fizzty-Buzz." If you're caught "Buzzing" or "Fizzing" when you shouldn't be, or saying a number rather than the required "Buzz" or "Fizz," you get to relax while the others continue.

BIZZ-BUZZ
• For yet another variation with the same effect as the above, try three and seven.
• The winner should probably take a nap!

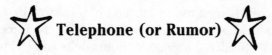

☆ Telephone (or Rumor) ☆

Number of Players: The more the better
Equipment: None

LORE
Here is a game that makes clever use of one of people's oldest foibles—the ability to misunderstand anything!

SETTING UP
• Players sit in a circle, within whispering distance of each other.

HOW TO PLAY
• The first player whispers a sentence of his or her choosing into the ear of the person to the left, who then whispers it to the person on his or her left, and so on around the circle.
• The last player then says the sentence, as he or she heard it, aloud. It's usually much different from the original!
• The second person then whispers a sentence, and so on until it's time to play another game.

Blind Man's Buff

Number of Players: 3 or more
Equipment: Blindfold

LORE

The pedigree of this game extends back to the fourteenth century. There's a reference to it in 1565 as "Hoodman Blind," which suggests that a hood rather than a blindfold was used in days past. It is a game copiously referred to throughout literature: Shakespeare's Hamlet makes mention of it, and in 1664 Samuel Pepys records his wife and household playing the game until 4 A.M.! It was considered a game for both adults and children, and was much more violent than the one that is played today, at least in my neighborhood. In classical times referred to as The Brazen Fly, players used whips made of papyrus to hit the poor blindfolded (or hooded) player. It's still known in Italy today as Blind Fly. A gentler game passed down simultaneously was, with some scorn, described as being "played by girls."

SETTING UP

• Establish boundaries beyond which players may not go. A small room, or a small area in a larger one, is fine.
• Players form a circle.
• One player is "Blindman." He or she chooses a helper. The helper puts the blindfold on Blindman and leads him or her to the center of the circle.

HOW TO PLAY

• The helper turns Blindman around three times while all say the rhyme, then lets go and joins the other players, who all must tease and touch Blindman without being caught.

• Any player caught must replace Blindman, and the game begins again.

> Blind man, blind man,
> Sure you can't see?
> Turn round three times,
> And try to catch me.

> Turn east, turn west,
> Catch as you can,
> Did you think you'd caught me?
> Blind, blind man!

Variations

• Once a player is caught, Blindman must identify him or her. If he or she cannot, the player goes free.

If play should begin to get on the wild side, try either of these variations to calm things down a bit.

• Players sit in a circle, with Blindman in the center. Players count off, remembering their numbers. Blindman calls out two numbers, and those players must exchange places by going through the circle while Blindman tries to catch one of them to replace him or her and while the other players chant the rhyme. If players trade places successfully, the game begins again.

• Players stand in a circle with Blindman in the center. They walk around the circle while chanting the rhyme. Blindman then taps or claps three times and everyone stops. He or she then points in the direction of a possible replacement and asks that player to make a sound, such as barking like a dog or singing opera, which the player must do, voice disguised. If Blindman guesses the player's identity, he or she must then become Blindman for the next round.

☆ Truth or Consequences ☆

Number of Players: 6–8 ideal
Equipment: Paper and pencil(s), 2 containers

LORE
A similar game, called Forfeits, was well known in Victorian times—it seems those Victorians really knew how to amuse themselves. Truth or Consequences is one of those games that is fun at parties, and fun for your family too.

SETTING UP
Though this game takes a bit of preparation, it's well worth the effort. If done in good spirits, the preparation can be part of the fun.
• Questions, with correct answers, are written on separate slips of paper and put into a Question Box. Include easy questions and difficult (but fair) ones, and try to assemble a wide range of topics: academic, personal, funny, trivial, nature—with an emphasis, of course, on whatever is interesting to the players.
• Now assemble a collection of "consequences," each again written on a separate slip of paper and put into a Consequences Box. Make them funny, silly, ridiculous, absurd—but not truly embarrassing.
• Another way to accomplish this is to have each player whisper one question and answer and one consequence for you to write (or have players write themselves if they can). Give the questions, answers, and consequences a quick scan for accuracy and appropriateness.
• Players form two equal-size teams (more if there are many children). Each team decides on the order in which players will take a turn.
• Last, draw up a score sheet, headed by team names.

HOW TO PLAY
• If two teams are playing, the first player from Team 2 chooses a question for the first player from Team 1 to answer. If the player from Team 1 answers correctly, that team receives five points. If the answer is incorrect, the question goes back into the Question Box without the answer having been revealed. Should the player from Team 2 get that question in later play, he or she should request a new question. The player who answered incorrectly must choose a slip from the Consequences Box and perform the consequence on it.

WINNING
• Although winning this particular game is almost beside the point, the team with the most points after all the questions are answered wins.

HINTS
• Team decisions and answers are allowed, but if they are wrong, team consequences must be performed!
• Here are some questions and consequences to get you started:

   Who was the first President of the United States?
   (George Washington)
   How much is 6 × 6? (36)
   What is a baby elephant called? (a calf)
   Without looking, what color shoes is (name of player) wearing?
   (That depends!)
   Who wrote down the Ten Commandments? (Moses)

Consequences
   Pat your head and rub your belly at the same time. (If that's too easy add deep knee bends.)
   Act like a monkey.
   Sing your favorite song.
   Imitate your mother or father scolding you.

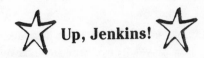

Up, Jenkins!

Number of Players: 6, 8, 10
Equipment: Quarter, table

LORE
This game had a surge of popularity in the 1930s. I've simplified the method of scoring a bit from the original, but I've included the original form in the *Variation* section for the purists among you. A good party game.

SETTING UP
• Players form two equal teams. A leader is chosen for each team.
• Teams either stand or sit facing each other across a table.
• The first team leader takes the coin.

HOW TO PLAY
• The coin is passed from hand to hand beneath the table (out of sight) until the leader of the second team calls "Up, Jenkins!"
• Players of the first team must hold their fists up in the air (one of the fists has the coin, of course).
• The leader of the second team then calls "Down, Jenkins!" and all fists must come down on the table, palms down flat (the coin is still concealed).
• The second team consults with each other to determine which hand conceals the coin. When a decision is reached, the team leader taps the suspect hand and says, "Up, Jenkins!" The tapped hand must then be raised. If the leader fails to say "Up, Jenkins" the player must not raise the hand. If the player does, the opposing team gets a free look.

WINNING
• If, lo and behold, the coin is under the tapped hand, the second team scores a point and gets to hold the coin for the next round.
• If there is no coin in that hand, the first team scores the point and gets to keep the coin for the next round.
• Often three guesses are given to a team before the round is declared over. Points can be arranged accordingly.
• The first team to get to a designated number of points, perhaps ten or twenty, wins.

Variation
Here is the original method of scoring:
• The team holding the coin is the only one that can score.
• The opposing team must guess the whereabouts of the coin but must try *not* to uncover it. This means that the opposing team must choose hands, one by one, to come off the table (by saying "Up, Jenkins!") until the hand concealing the coin is lifted.
• The number of hands left on the table are then counted, and the team with the coin scores the number of points equal to the number of hands left.
• The first team to reach a designated score (arrange this according to the number of players and their spans of concentration) wins.

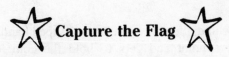

Capture the Flag

Number of Players: Many
Equipment: Various articles of clothing and small objects, chalk

LORE

In the *really* old days this was probably called War. Later children's adaptations called for using a handkerchief as the "flag," but nowadays it seems just about any possession is fair game.

SETTING UP

• Allow for running room.
• Two leaders each pick sides.
• A chalk dividing line is made between the sides.
• All players drop something belonging to them in their own team's territory.

HOW TO PLAY

• Members of each team either organize raiding parties or go it alone to capture the other team's possessions while at the same time trying to guard their own from "liberation."
• Any player who is caught on the opponent's side is taken prisoner and whatever "booty" he or she has is taken. Members of the prisoner's team must rescue the prisoner before any further raiding can take place.

WINNING

• The game ends either when one team has taken all the members of the other team prisoner or when one team has captured all of the other team's property.

4

Classic Games for Ages Eight to Ten

At around the age of eight to ten, you'll see that your child has developed a rather nice mix of games to play alone, with a friend, or in a group, and a combination of intellectually stimulating, skill-oriented, and physically challenging activities. Group games are largely played in teams, and there is mental as well as physical competition.

Speaking of competition, there is much going on in your child's life at this age—with much more to come. Reinforcing the idea of fun for its own sake and the rewards of relaxing, sportsmanlike play can remind you both that to enjoy childhood is good practice for enjoying life.

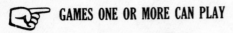 **GAMES ONE OR MORE CAN PLAY**

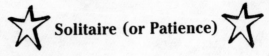

Solitaire (or Patience)

Number of Players: 1
Equipment: Playing cards

LORE
There is some mystery attached to the origin of playing cards. Though they may have been developed in China, there are differences between Chinese and European playing cards that indicate they may have developed independently in the European countries. We do know, however, that they existed in Europe as early as 1370, much as they are today. Solitare and Patience are the general names for these card games.

SETTING UP
Klondike is a very popular version of Solitaire. It is easy to play and fast moving.
• Discard the jokers. Aces rank low. The objective of the most simple of Solitaire games is to build "families," or suits of cards, onto base cards, or foundations.

HOW TO PLAY
• Deal out a row of seven cards. Place the first card face up, all others facedown.
• Beginning with the second card, deal a row on top of the first row, with the first card of this second row face up, the rest facedown.
• Beginning with the third card, do the same as above, and continue for all seven cards, until what you have looks like this:

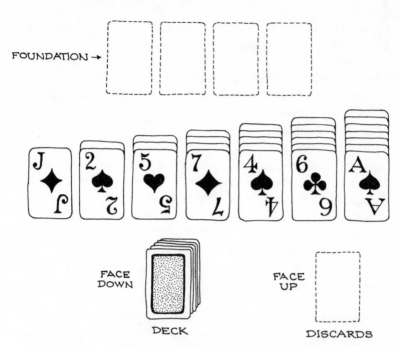

• If there are any aces visible, place them in a separate row, above the seven card piles, and turn the card underneath face up. If not, place the aces above as they become available for play. These are your "foundation" cards, upon which the rest of the cards are placed in ascending order.

• The seven small piles of cards act as sources from which to build the four suits of cards, in ascending order, on your foundation of aces.

• Scan the seven piles for cards that can be moved to the foundation. If you move any, the card beneath it can be turned over and becomes available for play. If the card you move is in the first pile and there is none beneath it, or if all the cards in one pile go to the foundation, see if you have a king available for play. A king can fill an empty space. If you have no king available immediately, wait until you turn one over, or come to one as you flip through the pack.

• If there is nothing that can go directly to the foundation, look among the seven piles and see whether any of the cards can be moved to any other pile. In order to do this, cards must alternate color (suit doesn't matter) as well as be in descending order. For example, if there is a red five on pile 3 and a black four on pile 5, the four may be placed on the five, and the card formerly beneath the four is turned face up. Arrange your card piles so that you can always see the first overturned card as well as the later additions to help you to see "sequences" you can move.

• Once all of your moves between piles are exhausted, you will probably have one or more "sequences," or groups of two or more cards on a pile in descending order and alternating color. Once you have a sequence, it can only be moved as a whole; it cannot be broken up.

• Your next source of material is the remainder of the deck. Cards in the deck can be turned over one at a time and placed either directly on the foundation or on any of the seven piles in which they will fit. The deck can be gone through only once. Cards that are not playable are placed face up in a separate pile. The top card of this pile is always available for play.

• Any time the last card in a pile can be put on the foundation, do so. Never take a card from your foundation to build onto the sequences in your piles. The object of the game is to build four complete suits on the foundation.

• If you have a king with a sequence on a card pile and a space opens up, the king and its entire sequence can be moved to the empty space in order to free the cards beneath.

• Play continues until the pack is gone through and no further moves are possible. Of course, you can always cheat and go through the pack more than once!

WINNING

- A player wins when all four suits on the foundation are complete.
- Shuffle well before the next game. I'll bet you can't play just once!

Variation

- If you elect to go through the deck by threes, you can go through more than once.

Just Plain Ball

Number of Players: 1 and up
Equipment: Spaldeen, wall optional

LORE

I have no name for this ball game, although games like Russia and Wall Ball are very similar. I do know, however, that it was very popular in my neighborhood, and just as much fun to play alone as with a group!

SETTING UP

- If there is more than one player, each should have his or her own ball, and take turns.
- If the player is playing against a wall, he or she should stand a comfortable distance away from it.

HOW TO PLAY

- The ball is thrown, either straight up into the air or against a wall. Establish a rhythm. Tasks are performed and the ball is caught for as many tasks as the player can accomplish without missing. Tasks must be done in order.

• Here are the tasks:

Meensies: Throw the ball against the wall and catch it before it bounces.

Clapsies: Throw the ball against the wall, clap, and catch the ball before it bounces.

Roll around: Throw the ball against the wall, revolve your hands around each other three times, and catch the ball before it bounces.

Tabacksies: Throw the ball against the wall, touch your back behind your shoulders with both hands, catch the ball before it bounces.

Right hand: Throw the ball against the wall with the right hand, catch it with the same hand before it bounces.

Left hand: Throw the ball against the wall with the left hand, catch it with the same hand before it bounces.

Highs-a-tude: Throw the ball against the wall as high as you can, catch it before it bounces.

Lows-a-tude: Throw the ball against the wall as low as you can, catch it before it bounces.

Touch your knees: Throw the ball against the wall, touch your knees, catch the ball before it bounces.

Touch your heel: Throw the ball against the wall, touch your heel, catch the ball before it bounces.

Touch your toe: Throw the ball against the wall, touch your toe, catch the ball before it bounces.

And under we go: Lift your leg, throw the ball under the leg to hit the wall, and catch the ball before it bounces.

• For the next round, double anything you can, after that triple, after that, take a rest!

Variations

There are many variations to this game—you may even want to add some of your own.

• For "clapsies" clap your hands once in front of you, once in back.
• **Turn around:** Throw the ball against the wall, turn around, catch the ball before it bounces.
• **Cross your heart:** Throw the ball against the wall, clap, cross your arms over your chest, clap again, catch the ball before it bounces.
• After going through the series once, go through again, throwing and catching with the right hand only, then with the left hand only.

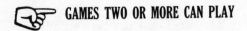 **GAMES TWO OR MORE CAN PLAY**

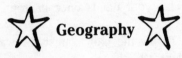 **Geography**

Number of Players: 2 or more
Equipment: None

LORE
This game is a schoolteacher's dream. It's challenging enough to make a child keep thinking, able to be built upon gradually and with repetition, and, mostly, just plain, interesting fun.

HOW TO PLAY
• One player begins by naming a city in the United States and the state it is in.
• The next player must take the last letter of the *city* named and think of another city in the United States that begins with that letter, then follow it with the state it is located in. For example: Player 1 says Fairbanks, Alaska. Player 2 may say San Francisco, California. Player 3 must then come up with a city beginning with the letter O, and so on.
• Cities can be used only once.

WINNING
• As play gets increasingly difficult, the number of points earned increases with each correct city and state. The first player gets one point for his or her answer, the second player gets two, and

so on. When a turn is missed or passed, the next player takes the turn, but the player who missed is allowed to try when his or her turn comes up again.
• The player with the most points at the game's end wins.

Variation
• This can also be played as an elimination game.
• More sophisticated players may want to take on the world!

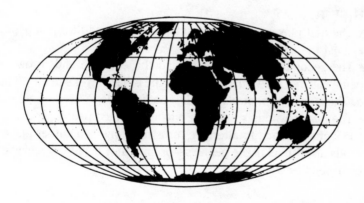

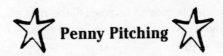

Penny Pitching

Number of Players: 2 or more
Equipment: 10 pennies each, flat surface near wall, chalk

LORE
We know this game has been around at least since Shakespeare's time, and most likely before that as pennies are not an absolute necessity—nuts, rocks, beads, or any number of things may be substituted. What with affluence today, however, you may see your children throwing quarters around—if not silver dollars.

SETTING UP
• Draw boundaries next to a wall, about four feet apart. Extend the lines approximately six feet and close with a line parallel to the wall. This is your pitching corridor.

HOW TO PLAY
• The first player stands behind the end line and throws a penny against the wall.
• The second player stands behind the end line and throws a penny against the wall, trying to hit the other player's penny. If he or she succeeds, that player takes both pennies.
• The player who has just won pitches the next penny.
• Players continue to alternate turns until one or another player winds up with all of the pennies—or until they decide to see what their pennies will buy!

Variations
There are innumerable variations to this game. Here are a few:
• A player wins if his or her penny falls within an agreed-upon distance from opponent's penny—a handspan, a number of inches, the length of a specific stick.

• A player wins only if his or her penny lands on or covers another player's penny.
• A pattern of numbered boxes may be drawn next to the wall. Pennies must land in the boxes to score the number of points in the box. Whoever gets to an agreed-upon score first wins.
• Pennies are thrown with the object of landing closest to the wall. The player whose penny lands closest to the wall wins all the pennies in that round.

Tiddlywinks

Number of Players: 2–6
Equipment: Small cups, tiddlywinks, flat surface

LORE
What game book would be complete without the classic of classic children's games—Tiddlywinks? Though your older child may dismiss it as a "baby" game, once you describe how to make a wink act tiddly by "squidging," and the pleasures and dangers of "squopping," a good time is almost guaranteed.

SETTING UP
• A flat surface is needed. A tabletop is perfect. However, be sure it is covered to prevent nicks and scratches. The floor, perhaps covered as well, is good too.
• Old-fashioned Tiddlywink sets are harder to come by these days since the advent of a nameless toy company's "reinterpretation" of the game. What you'll need, however, are six small, round, flat discs for each player—some Bingo games utilize them. These are the "winks." You may want to mark them a little differently for each player, to avoid confusion later. One larger flat

disc, known as the "squidger," is needed for each player, too. If your household does not yield such materials, we've found that pennies and quarters will do fine. A low cup—you can cut a paper cup down to a height of about 2 inches—is also needed for play.

• Set the cup in the middle of the table or play area. Each player then lines the "winks" up about six inches between him or her and the cup.

HOW TO PLAY

• Each player in turn "squidges" a wink by pressing its edge with the edge of the "squidger," making it leap "tiddly" (or tipsily) into the air. The player to get his or her wink closest to the cup then goes first. Turns then proceed clockwise.

• Each player's goal is to land the wink inside the cup, where it is safely out of play and is worth one point.

• If the wink lands inside the cup, the player takes another turn, until he or she misses.

• If, however, the wink misses the cup, it remains where it lands and the next player makes his or her attempt.

• Winks are played from wherever they landed last. If they should be "squidged" off the table, they are replaced on the table edge, closest to where they fell off.

• Should one player's wink land on another player's, that wink is said to be "squopped" and cannot move until the player on top moves his or her wink, or until the first player frees it by "squidging" another of his or her winks and knocking the top wink off.

WINNING

• The first player to "squidge" all of his or her winks into the cup and avoids being "squopped" or "squops" his or her opponents so they can't—oh, never mind.

Ghost

Number of Players: 2 to many
Equipment: None

LORE
This one will give your child's vocabulary and spelling ability a workout!

SETTING UP
• Players sit comfortably in a circle. Turns go clockwise.
• Words must have more than three letters.

HOW TO PLAY
• The first player thinks of a word and says the first letter of that word, such as *C* (for *crystal*).
• The next player must come up with a word of more than three letters that begins with *C*. He or she then says the second letter, such as *A* (*cattle*).
• The next player must then come up with a word of more than three letters that begins *CA*. He or she then says the third letter, such as *S* (*castle*). The object is to keep the word going for as long as possible and not be the player who completes it.
• Turns continue until one player cannot avoid completing a word. (Don't complete a word inadvertently as a player above would have if he or she had been thinking of the word "candle" and had said *N* to finish the word *can*.)
• A player who completes a word must take on one of the letters of the word *ghost*—and is said to have lost one life. The first time a player completes a word he or she takes *G*, the second time, *H*, and so on until the word *ghost* is complete. The player must then drop out of play.

• If a player cannot think of a word, he or she may try to bluff by saying any letter. If, however, the other players suspect the bluff, the player may be challenged and must either produce a word or lose a life!

• Once a word is complete, the next player in the circle chooses a word to begin the round.

WINNING

• The last player left wins.

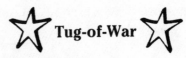

Tug-of-War

Number of Players: 2 upward
Equipment: Rope

LORE

Who said brute strength never settled anything? Cavepeople may not have played this as a game, but you can be certain the concept has been around since time immemorial. Seems to me I've even seen animals play Tug-of-War. Give yours plenty of room and a soft spot to land. This can be a game in itself or a way to settle the outcome of a tie. Though much younger children can play, it seems to engender real satisfaction in the eight- to ten-year age group. Players can attack with gusto, aggression has an acceptable outlet, and team spirit prevails.

SETTING UP

• Two evenly matched teams are chosen. Teams line up with leaders facing each other and team members one behind another in a straight line.

• Draw a line equidistant between the two team leaders, who should be about three feet apart.

• Each team member then takes hold of a portion of rope, leaving a comfortable amount of space in between members.

HOW TO PLAY
• Leaders say "Ready, set, go" and each team tries to pull the other over the middle line.

WINNING
• The first team to overpower the other and get the team leader over the line wins.

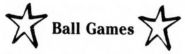

Ball Games

Number of Players: 2 to many
Equipment: Ball(s)

LORE
Balls are truly a universal, if not *the* universal, toy. Greek and Latin poets refer to ball games of their times. Homer describes "maidens" playing with a ball, and our old friend Ovid—remember him from Marbles?—remarked on the proclivity of Roman children to play with balls in the spring.

So prevalent did balls and ball games figure as a part of youth that in Stuart times (1603–1714), a guard with a whip would chase naughty "Boys with Toys and Balls" who dared to play near London's Royal Exchange.

Balls for play have certainly been around for a long time, but it wasn't until the advent of rubber in 1839 that the possibilities of ball games expanded to include younger children and the high-flying variations we're accustomed to today. Before there was rubber, balls were made of wood, cork, or leather stuffed with various, usually heavy, materials. Some American Indians made balls by wrapping strips of bark and smearing them with gum and sap from trees—yecch! I'm sure, however, that they had as much fun with them as children and adults of all ages do today. Here are some classic ball games to get you started.

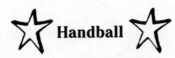

Handball

Number of Players: 2 or 4
Equipment: Handball, Spaldeen or tennis ball, wall, chalk

LORE
Generally considered to have originated in Ireland, Handball came full-blown to the United States around 1840. One of the distinctive features of this game is its spectrum of appeal. Handball is as well known in the street and playground as it is in the boardroom and at the club. It is played at all levels, at all ages, and *always* with passion.

SETTING UP
The game described here is a one-wall game.
• Wall should be approximately twenty feet wide by fifteen to twenty feet high. Court depth should extend approximately forty feet. It's best to play on a court that has a wire backstop and sides, if possible.
• Two lines are drawn on the ground parallel to the wall:
Short line: Fifteen to twenty feet from wall. A served ball, to be good, must bounce on the player's side of this line.
Long line: The rear boundary of the court, about forty feet from the wall, with sidelines extending another few feet beyond.
There is also an imaginary **service line** about ten feet forward of the short line.

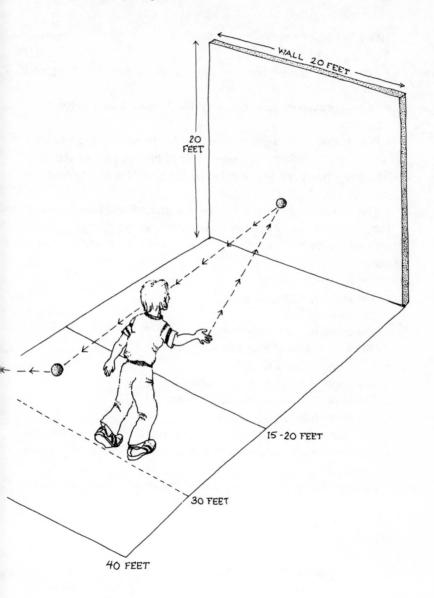

WALL 20 FEET

20 FEET

15-20 FEET

30 FEET

40 FEET

HOW TO PLAY
Serving
• The server stands between the sidelines and the short and service lines.

• The opponent stands between the sidelines and behind the short line.

• For doubles, the server's partner stands *outside* the sidelines and enters the court only when the ball bounces in fair territory. The two opponents stand between the sidelines and behind the short line.

• The server bounces the ball on the ground and hits it against the wall with the flat of his or her palm with a swinging stroke and follow-through, much as if the server's arm were a tennis racket.

• The server serves again if:

a. the serve is short;

b. the serve is long;

c. the serve hits the opponent;

d. the ball is missed altogether.

• The server loses a turn if:

a. the serve goes outside the sidelines;

b. the serve hits the server or partner;

c. the serve hits any obstruction;

d. the serve is the second short or second long one, or the second miss, or if one short and one long serve are served in succession;

• The server continues to serve until the server or partner misses a return shot.

• In doubles, both players on one team serve, then the two opponents serve.

Returning the Ball
• The ball can bounce once beyond the short line in the court, then it may be hit with the open palm back to the wall by the opponent. Opponents, or teams, alternate returning the ball.

• The **volley.** The ball can be hit before it bounces and must rebound fairly into the court.

• When the receiving side fails to return the ball, the same server serves again. When the serving side fails, the server is out and the serve passes to the opponent.

• Only the serving side can score points. One point is scored for every miss by the opponent.

• **Hinders** or **interferences** must be called when they occur.

a. If the ball hits an opponent before touching the wall, it must be served again.

b. If a player is intentionally blocked or interfered with by his or her opponent, the ball must be served again.

c. Interference from one's own partner doesn't count as a hinder.

d. Intentional blocking or interference is penalized by awarding one point to the offended player or team.

WINNING

• The first player or team to score either fifteen or twenty-one points (agree beforehand, please) wins. The winner must win by at least two points.

• A match is usually considered to be two out of three games.

 **Horse**

Number of Players: Best with 2
Equipment: Basketball and hoop

LORE
It isn't easy to make a claim of antiquity for a game that requires a basketball and hoop, but this one has been around long enough to join the ranks of classic pastimes. Parents are forewarned against dusting off their best shots and joining the competition without quick access to a good chiropractor.

SETTING UP
• Players decide order of turns.

HOW TO PLAY
• The first player makes any kind of shot. If he or she misses, the second player becomes the "leader."
• The second and all following players must make the same shot in the same way. The leader tries to make the most difficult or most ridiculous shots possible because . . .

WINNING
• If the following player misses, the first player gets the letter *H* and so on until one player spells "horse." That player is the winner.

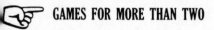

GAMES FOR MORE THAN TWO

Botticelli

Number of Players: 3 or more
Equipment: None

LORE
This game can actually be played by two people. However, it's such a brain drain, in my opinion, that it will last longer if there are more players to add their knowledge and wit to the pot. This one is a sharp and interesting game that will add to your fund of knowledge—or perhaps misinformation!

SETTING UP
• The first player thinks of either a person or a fictitious character to pretend to be. It must be one that he or she knows quite a bit about and one that the other players are also familiar with.

HOW TO PLAY
• The first player announces the first letter of the person's last name. For example, if the player is thinking of Tom Sawyer, he or she says "*S*."
• The other players must then guess who the first player is pretending to be.
• In order to do this, players may ask two types of questions. The first is the indirect question, which anyone can ask at any time. In order to ask an indirect question, a player must have in mind someone whose last name begins with the letter in question. He or she may inquire, "Are you a rock musician?" to which the first player must answer, "No, I'm not Bruce Springsteen" (or some

other rock musician with the last initial S). If the first player suspects, however, that his questioner is bluffing—that is, doesn't have anyone in mind at all—then the first player can challenge. Should the questioner be unable to come up with anyone, the matter is dropped, and the next question asked. If, however, the questioner had a legitimate person in mind and the *first* player cannot think of a rock musician whose last name begins with S, then the questioner gets to ask the second type of question, a direct one.

• A direct question must be answerable by yes or no. Such a question might be "Are you a fictitious character?" "Are you a woman?" "Are you alive?"

WINNING

• When a player thinks he or she has the answer, either an indirect question so specific it must be answered with the revelation or a direct question can be asked. For example, "Is your name in the title of a book written by Mark Twain?" surely must be answered with "Yes, I am Tom Sawyer." Or else "Are you Tom Sawyer?" can hardly be evaded.

• The player who first guesses the identity in question chooses whom he or she will pretend to be for the next round.

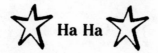

Ha Ha

Number of Players: 5 and up
Equipment: None

LORE
This one, I believe, is a new classic, spawned sometime in the 1950s when adults began to act silly at suburban parties. Whatever its pedigree, however, it is a lot of fun and still a good way to—as they say—break the ice.

SETTING UP
• The first person lies down on the floor, tummy side up, arms at sides, legs together, please.
• The second person lies down perpendicular to the first with his or her head resting on first person's stomach, in the same position as above.
• The third person lies down so that his or her head rests on second person's stomach, and so on, until everyone is on the floor.
• The first person says "Ha." The second person says "Ha, ha." The third person says "Ha, ha, ha." The fourth person—you get the idea, until everyone's head is bouncing on everyone else's stomach and everyone is laughing hysterically at this awfully silly game that is quite hilarious!

Charades

Number of Players: 4 and up
Equipment: Pencils, paper, container, watch

LORE
Charades, already an established and popular diversion in the eighteenth century, gained even more renown as the most popular of Victorian parlor games, celebrated in the literature of the time. Though it has had its ups and downs in terms of popularity over the years, it's still one of the best ways to bring out and satisfy the craving for high drama in all of us, and have a great time while doing it.

SETTING UP
• On a slip of paper, each player writes a word of at least two but usually three syllables, a book title, a movie title, the name of a television program, a proverb or saying ("Time flies," "All's well that ends well"), a play, or a song. Slips go into the container.
• Players form two teams of equal size.
• The first team chooses a slip of paper from the container and must act out, in mime, what the paper says. (To be sportsmanlike, the originator of the charade should remain silent if he or she recognizes it.)
• The first team may leave the room for up to five minues in order to plan their presentation strategy. When the players return they must first, in mime of course, identify the category they will act out. (See "Hints" below.) Each time the team goes on to the next syllable or the next word, the transition must be identified.
• As the first team gestures, the second team must try to guess what the first is trying to say. Close or correct guesses are encouraged by the first team by beckoning gestures and/or nodding. Wrong guesses are dismissed by "halt" signal, head shaking, or brushing-away motions.

• Time limit is five minutes. If the second team guesses correctly it receives a point. If the charade is not guessed by the time limit, the first team receives a point.

WINNING
• Whichever team has the most points when both teams are ready to quit wins.

HINTS
• If players are acting out a word, they first break it into syllables that are acted out separately, then put them together and act the entire word.

Here are some of the standard gestures to get you started:

Word: Arm bent at elbow, fist shown to audience, thumb and forefinger extended to show approximate length of word.
Book: Hands held side by side in front of eyes, palms flat, facing self.
Movie: One hand imitates camera lens in front of eye, other arm rotates from elbow like old-fashioned movie camera.
TV program: Hands describe shape of television screen, mime turning on the "on" knob.
Proverb or saying: Mime making quotation marks by raising hands, using index and middle finger in crooked position, other fingers folded around each other.
Play: Raise both hands, bring downward and spread with a flourish to represent the opening of a theater curtain.
Song: Mime singing.
Number of syllables or words: Hold up appropriate number of fingers.
Shorten: Index finger and thumb come closer together.
Stretch: Hands describe "pulling taffy" away from each other.

You can make up the rest!

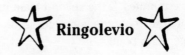

Ringolevio

Number of Players: 10 and up
Equipment: None

LORE
Although this is a bred-in-the-city game, it's easily adaptable to other locations, as long as there are a lot of "things" around to aid evasive action!

SETTING UP
• Players form two teams of even size, the "chasers" and the "runners."
• The site that acts as both "home base" and "jail" must be big enough to accommodate several players at once—a stoop or porch is good.

HOW TO PLAY
• Everyone begins at home base. The chasers count to ten while the runners scatter but do not hide.
• Chasers, either singly or in teams, try to catch runners who in turn try not to be caught by dodging, running, and using whatever obstructions lie in the way to stay out of reach of their would-be captors.
• If a runner is caught, the chaser must be able to hold on to him or her and say "Ringolevio, 1, 2, 3." If the runner doesn't break free before then, he or she is "captured" and must go meekly with the captor to jail.
• The captor of the first prisoner becomes the "jailer" and must stay at base guarding any other prisoners who are captured.
• Prisoners can be set free in one or more of the following ways:
   A prisoner can free him- or herself by running from the jail without being tagged by the jailer.

Another runner can tag the prisoner and say "Free." The prisoner must then escape without being tagged by the jailer. The free runner, if tagged, becomes a prisoner.

If more than one prisoner is caught, they can sit or stand so they are touching. If only one of them is touched by a free player, the others can go free as well by virtue of "electricity."

WINNING

• When all the runners are caught, the chasers have won. Now it's time to switch roles and begin again!

Spud

Number of Players: 10 and up
Equipment: Kickball or soccer ball

LORE

This isn't a game that you can win, but, oh boy, can you lose!

SETTING UP

• This game is played outdoors, in gymnasiums, or in other large spaces without breakables.
• Players stand in a group. "It" stands in center of group, holding the ball.

HOW TO PLAY

• "It" drops the ball and calls out a name. Everyone else scatters.
• The player whose name was called must catch the ball and call "Halt." Everyone freezes. The new "It" tries to hit another player with the ball from where he or she is standing. If "It" misses, everyone runs again while he or she recovers the ball, cries "Halt," and tries again.

• If "It" hits a player, he or she runs away and the hit player becomes the new "It," who must recover the ball and try to hit someone else.

• When a thrower misses, it's called a "Spud" and counts one against him or her. When a player is hit, that player also has a "Spud" against him or her. Now comes the good part.

• If a player collects three "Spuds," he or she must stand approximately twenty feet from the other players in the following position: facing away, hands on knees. This gives the other players a good target because now each player gets a shot at the hapless sport.

• Play is then begun again with a group in the center, the "Spudded-out" player being "It."

Variations

• In some versions of the game, the victim is allowed to fire back at his or her teammates, who must adopt the same position in anticipation of the throws.

• For younger children, you may (or may not) want to introduce the "Paddlewheel." The unfortunate who has "Spudded out" undergoes further indignity by having to crawl through the legs of the other players, who are lined up one behind the other. As he or she is crawling through on all fours, the others get to spank the crawling player—but not too hard.

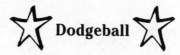

Dodgeball

Number of Players: As many as possible!
Equipment: Kickball or soccer ball

LORE
This is another lively game that shouldn't be played until the decks are cleared.

SETTING UP
• Players form two even groups. The first group forms a large circle. The second group stands scattered within.

HOW TO PLAY
• The members of the first group must hit the members of the second group with the ball. Members of the second group dodge, jump, and weave to avoid being hit. They can do anything but leave the circle.
• A hit player must join the circle.
• The ball is picked up by the person it is closest to in the first group. If the ball stops inside the circle, a center player may toss it back or a circle player may retrieve it, but it can't be thrown until that player returns to the circle.
• If two players are hit by one throw, the first player hit leaves the circle. If there is disagreement over who was hit first, settle the dispute with Odds and Evens.

WINNING
• The last player to remain in the center wins.
• The second group becomes the first and vice versa for the next game.

Keep Away

Number of Players: As many as possible
Equipment: Soccer ball

LORE
Though one of the simplest games imaginable, Keep Away is a
great challenge and will keep players going for long stretches at
a time. Just see to it that height is fairly distributed between
teams!

SETTING UP
• Players form two equal teams.
• Opponents pair up and scatter over the playing field.

HOW TO PLAY
• The ball is put into play from the center of the field.
• Each team tries to keep the ball away from the other team by
passing it to teammates. Each successful throw counts as one
point.
• Players keep count out loud.

WINNING
• The team to complete longest series of passes within a designated time limit wins.

REFERENCES

Bancroft, Jesse H. *Games.* New York: Macmillan, 1937.

Beaver, Patrick. *Victorian Parlor Games.* New York: Thomas Nelson, 1974.

Belton, John, and Cramblit, Joella. *Domino Games.* Wisconsin: Raintree Publishers, 1976.

Bett, Henry, M.A. *The Games of Children: Their Origin and History.* London: Methuen, 1929.

Brandreth, Gyles. *The World's Best Indoor Games.* New York: Pantheon, 1981.

Diagram Group. *The Way to Play.* London: Paddington Press, 1975.

Estrada, Billie. *How to Play Hopscotch: A Game Created by Children.* Greenville, SC: Agency Press, 1974.

Evans, Patricia. *Rimbles: A Book of Children's Classic Games, Rhymes, Songs and Sayings.* New York: Doubleday, 1961.

Ferretti, Fred. *The Great American Book of Sidewalk, Stoop, Dirt, Curb and Alley Games.* New York: Workman, 1975.

Gallagher, Rachel. *Games in the Street.* New York: Four Winds Press, 1976.

Glovach, Linda. *Little Witch's Black Magic Book of Games.* Englewood Cliffs, NJ: Prentice-Hall, 1974.

Gripki, Camilla. *Cat's Cradle, Owl Eyes: A Book of String Games.* New York: William Morrow, 1984.

Grunfeld, Frederic V., ed. *Games of the World.* New York: Ballantine Books, 1975.

Loeper, John J. *The Shop on High Street: The Toys and Games of Early America.* New York: Atheneum, 1978.

Mulac, Margaret E. *Town and Country Fun and Games.* New York: Harper, 1956.

Mulac, Margaret E., and Holmes, Marian S. *The School Game Book.* New York: Harper & Row, 1950.

Newell, William Wells. *Games and Songs of American Children.* New York: Dover Publications, 1963.

North, Robert. *Town and Country Games.* New York: Thomas Y. Crowell, 1947.

Opie, Iona and Peter. *The Oxford Nursery Rhymes Book.* New York: Oxford University Press, 1955.

Opie, Iona and Peter. *Children's Games in Street and Playground.* Oxford: The Clarendon Press, 1969.

Opie, Iona and Peter, eds. *The Oxford Dictionary of Nursery Rhymes.* Oxford: The Clarendon Press, 1952.

Temko, Florence, and Simon, Elaine. *Paperfolding to Begin With.* New York: Bobbs-Merrill, 1968.

INDEX